SOFT LANDING

AIRLINE INDUSTRY STRATEGY, SERVICE, AND SAFETY

_____

Andrew R. Thomas

Apress®

Soft Landing: Airline Industry Strategy, Service, and Safety

ISBN-13 (pbk): 978-1-4302-3677-1

ISBN-13 (electronic): 978-1-4302-3678-8

Trademarked names may appear in this book. Rather than use a trademark symbol with every occurrence of a trademarked name, we use the names only in an editorial fashion and to the benefit of the trademark owner, with no intention of infringe-ment of the trademark.

Lead Editor: Jeff Olson
Editorial Board: Steve Anglin, Mark Beckner, Ewan Buckingham, Gary Cornell,
  Jonathan Gennick, Jonathan Hassell, Michelle Lowman, James Markham,
  Matthew Moodie, Jeff Olson, Jeffrey Pepper, Frank Pohlmann, Douglas
  Pundick, Ben Renow-Clarke, Dominic Shakeshaft, Matt Wade, Tom Welsh
Coordinating Editor: Jennifer L. Blackwell
Copy Editor: Mary Behr
Compositor: Mary Sudul
Indexer: SPi Global
Cover Designer: Anna Ishschenko

Distributed to the book trade worldwide by Springer-Verlag New York, Inc., 233 Spring Street, 6th Floor, New York, NY 10013. Phone 1-800-SPRINGER, fax 201-348-4505, e-mail orders-ny@springer-sbm.com, or visit www.springeronline.com.

For information on translations, please contact us by e-mail at info@apress.com, or visit www.apress.com.

Apress and friends of ED books may be purchased in bulk for academic, corporate, or promotional use. eBook versions and licenses are also available for most titles. For more information, reference our Special Bulk Sales–eBook Licensing web page at www.apress.com/bulk-sales.

Other Books By Andrew R. Thomas

Aviation Insecurity: The New Challenges of Air Travel

Air Rage: Crisis in the Skies

Aviation Security Management, 3 volumes

Change or Die! (with M. David Dealy)

Defining the Really Great Boss (with M. David Dealy)

Direct Marketing in Action (with Dale Lewison, William Hauser, and Linda Orr)

The Distribution Trap (with Timothy Wilkinson)

The Final Journey of the Saturn V (with Paul Thomarios)

Global Manifest Destiny (with John Caslione)

Growing Your Business in Emerging Markets (with John Caslione)

Managing By Accountability (with M. David Dealy)

New World Marketing (with Timothy Wilkinson)

The Rise of Women Entrepreneurs (with Jeanne Halladay-Coughlin)

Supply Chain Security, 2 volumes

Para Hilma de Pastor: una gran madre para mi esposa, una buena abuela para mis niños y una viajera excelente.

Contents

About the Author

Andrew R. Thomas is a bestselling business writer and assistant professor of international business at the University of Akron. His recent book, *The Distribution Trap*, was awarded the Berry-American Marketing Association Prize for the Best Book of 2010. Thomas is founding editor-in-chief of the *Journal of Transportation Security* and contributing editor at *Industry Week*. He has been interviewed by more than 1,000 media outlets and is a regularly featured analyst for CNBC, FOX News, and NBC. A multimillion-mile flier, he has traveled to and conducted business in more than 120 countries on all seven continents.

Acknowledgments

Every book I have ever written is ultimately a debt that can never fully be repaid to the many people whose thoughts and writings my own rest upon.

My more intimate debts are to the people who have helped me to craft this work. Greg Dumont was the person who first saw this book for what it could be. My other colleagues at the University of Akron, including Ravi Krovi, Bill Baker, Marie David, Deborah Owens, Doug Hausknecht, and Bill Hauser, have fostered my growth as a writer and researcher more than any scholar deserves. The conversations with Yara Asad provided tremendous insight into the very human notions of contradiction and imperfection. Brian Sullivan and Steve Elson are true comrades and patriots who are willing to help at every turn. My great friends Paul Thomarios and Craig Vinkovich are always ready to share an intriguing thought. My mentor Tim Wilkinson has shown me the road ahead and, more importantly, how to best live it as a person of character. My parents instilled in me a sense of exploration from an early age and for this I am eternally grateful. My grandmother and sisters are the kinds of unconditional supporters one can only dream of. My long-time editor Jeff Olson knows instinctively how to manage my moods and fears. My children, Paul Bryan, and Alana, motivate me to leave behind a better world than the one I was blessed to inherit. And, finally, my wife Jacqueline is always at my side.

The Past

In Joseph Heller's *Catch-22*, there is the following exchange between the anti-hero Yossarian and the unwavering mind of military authority:

> *Major Danby replied indulgently with a wide superior smile,*
> *"But, Yossarian, what if everyone felt that way?"*
> *"Then I'd certainly be a damned fool to feel any other way, wouldn't I?"*

Through his distinct prose, Heller reveals to us that those who need or want to think for themselves will always be a minority. That the contrarian is always fighting an uphill battle against conventional wisdom.

So might be the case of this book as well...

You Cannot Be Serious!

"The enemy of the good is the perfect."

—Voltaire

It wouldn't take much to categorize modern air travel as an experience somewhere between juvenile detention and dread. Recently, I caught a CNN headline story that hysterically reported that 2,600 pieces of luggage are lost each day by the airlines in America. Two thousand six hundred! In feet, that's almost half a mile. In years, it takes us back to the construction of the Hanging Gardens of Babylon by King Nebuchadnezzar. 2,600 lost bags every day: that's almost 1 million annually!

Around that same time, a YouTube clip of a six year-old girl getting a police-like "pat down" by a TSA screener began making the rounds. The video was shot and posted by the girl's father, who, along with his wife, were forced to stand by, helpless, as their daughter was touched in uncomfortable ways and places. Dishearteningly, scenes like this one involving other small children, paralyzed war heroes, or elderly people in wheelchairs are not uncommon.

If you've flown in the last year or so, you've found that boarding a flight has gotten even worse, as more and more of us carry on all of our stuff to avoid the airlines' innovative program of charging for checked bags. God help you if you're one of the last people to enter the cabin and need space in the overhead bin.

Between the continuous stream of media reports about lousy customer service, the dehumanizing security checkpoints, and the cattle-class experience, one might wonder why anyone would ever want to fly at all. It seems that air travel today is something for the masochistic or those with no other options.

Yet I disagree with how many in the media and the government, as well as my fellow passengers, might characterize air travel and the industry today. I am a contrarian. Let me put my cards on the table right up front: I think the airline industry, unvarnished and with warts and all, is one of the best things we have going for us. I look at the 2,600 lost bags a day with awe—but for a different reason than most folks might. In May of 2011, for example, more than 49 million passengers flew in the U.S. Of those, more than 172,000 reported that the airline lost their luggage.[1] This means that there is somewhere around a 0.35% chance that you would have lost your bag if you flew commercial that month—or a 99.65% likelihood the bag would have arrived with you. And while the TSA and the behavior of some of its agents are sometimes questionable and occasionally reprehensible, the agency screens nearly 2 million passengers and their carry-ons each day, which is about the same number as the entire population of Houston. And, despite the fact that the flying experience has become much more like going to Wal-Mart or taking the bus, the average cost of a ticket has fallen by more than half in real dollars over the past twenty years.

My point here is not to justify the behavior of the industry and the government at every turn: to the contrary. Take a look at my earlier books, articles, and public comments about the industry and you'll find I've been highly critical of the ways the airlines' leaders and the federal government have managed themselves and treated the traveling public—the people who ultimately pay their salaries and underwrite the system. Let's be frank, they're easy targets, especially if we focus on the outliers. As a business professor, I can assure you that there are only a handful of successful case studies in the airline industry: Southwest comes to mind, and almost no one else. In fact, the industry provides countless examples of what *not* to do when trying to manage an enterprise. On the governmental front, the bungling by Congress, FAA, and TSA when it comes to overseeing the airline industry is the stuff of legend. Still, I am an optimist—a rational one, I believe—when it comes to the airline industry. Bluntly stated: It's certainly not perfect, but it's pretty darn good.

---

[1] U.S. Department of Transportation, Aviation Consumer Protection Division, "Air Travel Consumer Report," July 2011, http://airconsumer.ost.dot.gov/reports/atcr11.htm.

How Can You Say That?!

I am not a shill. I don't work for anyone associated with the industry and never have. I'm pretty sure after this book is published, any friends I may have in the industry will run for cover. My optimism comes from two places: first, as a frequent flier who has logged more than 3 million miles over the past 20 years; and, secondly, as a student of the industry for more than 15 years.

Probably like you, I have my own travel nightmares. Every now and then I enjoy comparing stories with my friends, seatmates, and students. Having spent my adult life logging at least 100,000 miles a year, I've had my share of trips to and/or from hell. I still remember them vividly and quietly wear them as a personal badge of honor. One in particular sticks out: a 54-hour slog from Madagascar to back home, which included 30 hours of delays.

Even though it was quite draining, I wasn't riding in a Higgins Boat to Omaha Beach. I was ensconced in the safest transportation system ever designed. And, while the delays were maddening at the moment, I completed the trip in about the same amount of time it would have normally taken the year I was born: 1967. Moreover, in the century before my birth, I would have had to make the journey by ship, which would have taken several weeks, and put me at the mercy of seasickness, pirates, tropical diseases, and only God knows what else. Finally, the cost—whether by air in 1967 or sea in the 19th century—would have been exponentially higher than what I paid.

Today we are beyond fortunate to have access to the global air transport network in its current form. As a middle-class guy, my historical equivalent would never have imagined the places I've been able to see because of the accessibility to the planet afforded to me by modern air travel. And I'm not an exception. Hundreds of millions of people, maybe billions, have been able to connect with the bigger world in ways no one conceived a mere 90 years ago. Experiencing the adventure of travel, enjoying the beauty of a family vacation, seeing an old friend or making new ones, celebrating a wedding out of town, visiting your grandchildren, or paying respects at a funeral—the important moments in life—are more achievable for more people than ever before in history. The availability of air travel makes this, and so much more, possible. Frankly, at this level, there is simply no disputing the fact that the airline industry is a tremendous benefit to so many of us.

At another level, the rational optimist in me is also aware of what the airline industry means for human progress and innovation. The evolutionary biologist Matt Ridley ties the advancement of human development to what he calls "ideas having sex." When people and their ideas come into contact with one another, adaptation and improvement often occur. Ridley asserts that it is collective innovation, fertilized by exchange, which fosters the great leaps in civilization.[2] When scientists from around the world travel to a conference to listen to one another share their research findings—and maybe have a few drinks together, too—wonderful things can happen. Ideas are shared; collective intelligence is unleashed; new innovations are born. When businesspeople travel to distant places to visit suppliers, customers, and prospects, the introduction of new technologies, products, and services happens. Exchange occurs and the wonderful unknown that is human creation gets fueled once again. It may sound a bit trite, but the airline industry facilitates the cross-pollination of ideas and human progress.

Of course, if you're reading this book while sandwiched between two fat guys on a cross-country trip, or waiting in a crowded terminal after your flight was cancelled, all this talk about memories, innovation, and progress might ring hollow. I readily admit the experience of flying today is a lot worse than it was in the past. And, unfortunately, the future looks no better. Going forward, as you'll see in this book, passengers can continue to expect over-packed planes, byzantine security practices, and fewer benefits than those given to guys serving six months for a parole violation. In addition, if you work for the airlines, the likelihood of better pay and benefits is quite low. Taxpayers should anticipate more bailouts and subsidies to the industry, as the airlines and the manufacturers of aircraft will always have their hands out. And, if you're a shareholder, good luck: profits and dividends will remain few and far between. Even so, what I am saying here is that on balance, despite all of the industry's imperfections that continuously plague its stakeholders, it remains a net positive for society. Access for more and more people to the air transport system overshadows corporate mismanagement, governmental waste, fraud, abuse, and awful customer treatment. In short, the benefits of more people enjoying their lives and exchanging ideas with each other far outweighs the costs and burdens put on us by the industry.

Contradiction and Imperfection

Contradiction is part of everyone and inherent within all human endeavors. I love tomato juice, a strong Bloody Mary, and extra sauce on my pizza. But I refuse to eat tomatoes on my salad. Thomas Jefferson, who wrote some of

---

[2] I would recommend Matt Ridley's book *The Rational Optimist: How Prosperity Evolves* (New York; Harper, 2010) without reservation.

the most profound words about equality in history, traveled with his slave to Paris and fathered several children with her. We are all hypocritical and contradictory—and imperfect—in various forms. From economics comes the Nirvana Fallacy. It occurs when we compare actual things with unrealistic, idealized alternatives. It refers to the somewhat natural human tendency to simplify complex things and seek implausible solutions. Recognizing this—and avoiding the trap—is a big part of what makes us adults. What keeps us immature, however, is when we expect perfection in others and will not tolerate any contradictions.

As we move forward, I will try to appeal to your better angels and humbly request that you try to remember not the few bad flights you have endured, but instead the dozens, and maybe hundreds, of uneventful ones that delivered you safe and sound. Once you do that, we can start our journey to critically and fairly assess the industry for what it is, what it is not, and what it realistically can be. As it says in the New Testament:

> "When I was a child, I spoke like a child.
> I understood as a child.
> But when I became a adult, I put away childish things."

When it comes to looking at the airline industry, we need to adult-up and appreciate what we have. Which brings me to the title of this book: *Soft Landing*. It is not merely an attempt to capture a short title that is easily recalled. The term derives from both economics and aviation. From an economics perspective, a soft landing is a slowdown in the business cycle that does not lead to a recession: a minor speed bump and little else. If you're a pilot, crewmember, or a passenger, a soft landing is just that: a smooth touchdown. I'm convinced that the airline industry, probably despite itself, is setting the stage for a period of sustained stability. This is *not* to say that constant profits are just around the corner for the industry. The industry has never really been profitable over the long term and no evidence suggests that it ever can be. Nor is it to say that the industry will never experience a massive downturn again, as it did in early 1992, September 2001, or, most recently, in 2008.

Instead, the focus of this book will be on what is happening in the industry that is creating an environment where the wild fluctuations of the past—characterized by short periods of profits followed by much longer spells of huge losses—are smoothed over and reduced. Instability, the natural opposite of stability, will remain, but it should be less frequent and devastating. The book acknowledges that while there will still be some unavoidable turndowns in the future, they won't be as low or as long lasting as the ones of the past; that the airline industry, whether through good planning, blind luck, or a combination of the two, is now entering an era where it finds itself more resilient, robust, and prepared for the inevitable turbulence than any time in recent memory. In the end, the industry will still have imperfections and contradictions. But, with some effort, they should be less in number and magnitude.

So Why Should You Care?

On the first day of each semester, I challenge my students—and, ultimately, myself—to ask the "So what?" questions: "You have been required to take this course by the university. Why? Why are we making you learn about concepts such as foreign direct investment and mercantilism? How do you think this relates to your ability to think critically, and how does it directly impact your future?" Whatever we do, these kinds of questions should be asked. I use them as a way to make sure the material I am teaching stays relevant to my audience. I am assuming that by reading this far, you have some degree of interest in the current and future state of the airline industry. With all due respect to your curiosity, let me go further and specifically articulate why you should care.

The scope of the airline industry is massive and its reach into our lives is equally impressive. In 2010, in the United States alone, 743 million passengers took a scheduled trip by air. This is almost two-and-a-half times the entire population of the country. Moreover, 536,000 Americans were employed full-time by the industry, about the same number as all of the residents currently living in Seattle.[3] Further, the direct annual contribution of the airline industry to the U.S. economy is approximately $781.5 billion, or more than 5% of America's total gross domestic product.[4] If we expand the impact of the industry to include other critical business sectors such as aircraft manufacturing, travel and tourism, retail, shipping, and international trade—each which are all dependent upon the airlines in big ways—the overall amount of U.S. GDP driven by the airline industry is over $1.2 trillion, or nearly 9%.[5] These numbers are similar to the contribution of the entire automotive sector in the U.S.[6]

---

[3] Air Transport Association and Bureau of Transportation Statistics.

[4] Federal Aviation Administration, "The Economic Impact of Civil Aviation on the U.S. Economy," (Washington, D.C.) December 2009.

[5] Ibid.

[6] Michael F. Thompson and Ali Arif Merchant, "Employment of Economic Growth in the U.S. Automotive Manufacturing Industry," *Indiana Business Review*, Spring 2010, www.ibrc.indiana.edu/ibr/2010/spring/article2.html.

At the global level, the numbers are just as compelling. In 2010, more than 2 billion passengers flew, which represents the equivalent of nearly 30% of all human beings alive today. They could have traveled on one of 1,629 airlines, which flew 27,271 aircraft, and used the facilities of 3,733 airports.[7] Moreover, nearly 32 million jobs are generated around the world by the industry and almost $4 trillion is contributed to global GDP.[8] Although it is not known for sure, it is likely that somewhere around 300 million individuals took a commercial flight somewhere in 2010. Even a cursory glance at Table 1-1 reveals the reach the global airline industry has into so many facets of society.

Table 1-1. Key Stakeholders in the Global Airline Industry

Manufacturers	Carriers	Directly Served
• Airframes/Engines • Mechanical systems • Computers/Electronics • Information systems • Software • Materials/Chemicals	• Major airlines • Regional airlines • Charter airlines • Special services • Air cargo carriers • General aviation	• Passengers • Rental cars/Parking • Other ground transport • Hotels/Restaurants • Tourism/Attractions • Retail • Travel Agents • Cruise lines • Conventions
Governments • Aviation authorities • Legislative bodies • Regulatory agencies • Customs • Air Traffic Control	GLOBAL AIRLINE INDUSTRY	**Employees** • Manufacturers • Airlines • Airports • Cargo • Aviation services • Bureaucrats
Aviation Services • Insurance • Leasing/Financing • Distributors • Telecommunications • Maintenance • Fuel and oil • Training • Universities	**Airports** • Major airports • General aviation airports • Training centers • Terminal maintenance • Catering/In-flight service • Air Traffic Control	**Cargo** • Freight forwarders • Warehousing • Consolidation • Mail • Transport

---

[7] International Air Transport Association, "Fact Sheet: Economic and Social Benefits of Air Transport," www.iata.org/pressroom/facts_figures/fact_sheets/Pages/economic-social-benefits.aspx.

[8] Ibid.

As the only truly worldwide transportation system, it is not a stretch to conclude that the global economy is driven at least partially by what happens in the skies. Beyond the 2 billion passengers, the airlines also transport billions of tons of cargo on the planes you and I fly in. What kind of cargo is moving? Items like mail, electronics, medicines, luxury goods, flowers, seafood, tropical fish, human remains, critical spare parts, and thousands of other things that make our lives better. All these passengers and all this cargo moves seamlessly over oceans, mountain ranges, and national borders 24/7/365 as a kind of coordinated orchestra that exceeds the individual genius of Bach or Mozart.

Beyond the numbers, the ubiquitous nature of the airline industry is something that many of us have already built into our lives. The real opportunity to take a flight to anywhere at almost a moment's notice is seared into our consciousness. It is something that we don't even think about. This knowledge and certainty about the unfettered availability and access we have to the world via the global airline network makes us dependent on it for our comfort and the day-to-day conduct of our lives—and all in a good way. Try to imagine your world without being able to fly. What would change? How would your view of things around you be altered? How about your business? Could it be done at all without the availability of air travel? If so, and you're probably one of the lucky few, how much harder would it be? And what about all of those important moments in your life? How many of them would not have happened at all if you couldn't have flown? My point in all of this is to recognize how indispensible—and I choose that word carefully—the airline industry is to our lives.

But Is It Really an Industry?

To call the airline industry an "industry" in the purest sense is probably disingenuous. The use of the term implies a commercial enterprise that operates under the conditions of normal business parameters. That includes the development of investments and a sufficient number of customers to whom its output can be sold for a profit on a *regular, consistent basis*. While the airline industry does regularly make investments and it has many customers, historically this has rarely translated into regular, consistent profits. In fact, since the advent of the airline industry, the amount of total losses has far outweighed any profits that may have been earned. Regular, consistent profits for the overall airline industry have never happened. There are a couple moments in time where profits were earned by all; and there have been a few airlines that turned a profit every year, but those are exceptions.

Since deregulation in 1978, the airline industry in the U.S. has lost around $60 billion in current dollars. There was a brief period of time during second half of the 1990s when the carriers did make some money. However, that was all washed away and then some in the period from 2000 till today. It was hardly any better before deregulation, when bankruptcies and consolidations clogged the landscape. Arguments have been made that factors like high taxes, rising fuel costs, weak demand, the entry of low-cost carriers, terrorism, geopolitical shifts, economic downturns, or something else is what keeps profits away. The logic seems to be that if the industry could better predict when one or more of these factors will rear their ugly heads, profitability would be there for the taking. But the assumption is hollow: how can anyone accurately predict what oil prices will be next year? Or when and how the next terrorist attack will occur and by whose hands? Or the prospects of economic growth or stagnation? Or the next major geopolitical shift?

From where I sit, the airlines have operated in a perpetually loss-driven environment in which the over-arching strategic objective is survival, and little else. As you'll see next in Chapter 2, the survivability of the airline industry has been tied to the huge amount of governmental support it has received since its inception. Take that away, and there would hardly be any kind of an airline industry to speak of, and certainly nothing we'd recognize today. This dependency on government may irritate the "free market" crowd, but a mature look at the airlines requires us to check our ideologies at the door. I will argue later that the rush to government bailouts for the banking, insurance, and automotive sectors during the panic of 2008 was possible only because the airlines had set the precedent in the wake of the 9/11 attacks. And that those industries in 2008 successfully followed the same approach the airlines used to get billions in handouts from the government in 2001—by deploying armies of lobbyists and leveraging irrational fears.

Stability: Our Best Hope

When I speak of stability as it relates to the airline industry, I mean it as the capacity to resist sudden deterioration. It is more than the survival mode the industry has habitually functioned in. Instead, it is resiliency and adaptation—and maybe even improvement—in the face of big changes and threats. I repeat: it doesn't mean profitability. I simply believe it is not possible for the industry to generate long-term, sustainable profits in its current form, and to change its current form is not even remotely a consideration.

Unfortunately, because of their exposure to so many factors that lie outside of their control, the airlines have traditionally counted on luck—and government largesse—more than anything else to get them through. While plans, forecasts, and strategic objectives are regularly written, developed, and pursued with strong attention to detail, it is the roller-coaster nature of the industry that ultimately determines how things play out: a sudden turn here—say oil prices spike because of a crisis in the Middle East—or a drop there, like an economic shock that suddenly keeps passengers away. By effectively being held hostage by so many things outside of their purview and being, by nature, pretty inflexible, when things go bad for the airlines, they go real bad. As you'll see later on, the turndown in early 1992, the recession of 2000, and the fallout from 9/11 each shook the industry more violently than it should have because the airlines possessed little or no room to maneuver. The industry was a prisoner to a system that had already set itself for up failure.

Darwin observed that it is the agile and the adaptable that survive—not the biggest and strongest—and the same is true for organizations. In the past, however, the airlines haven't displayed the kind of agility we would want as stakeholders. But things may be finally starting to change. Stability for the industry finally appears on the horizon. It is distant, but seeable nevertheless.

Finally, a New Era for the Airline Industry?

Having studied the airline industry since the mid 1990s, I have read my share of consultants' reports, op-eds, industry analyses, and the like that predicted the industry was ready to turn the corner and enter a new era of stability. Each one of these came up short in some way. It seems just when we think we've figured things out, something in the nature of the industry catches us by surprise. So you might wonder, in the face of all the failed predictions of the past, why I am going out on a limb now and saying that the industry is ready to experience a soft landing? My answers to this question make up the core of this book.

To start with, the soft landing is *not* because of globalization. In Chapter 3, I'll address the paradox of globalization and the industry. While the airline industry has been one of the pillars of the globalization over the past 50 years, the industry itself is mired in a hodge-podge of local political struggles and national idiosyncrasies. Even though airliners, with their nation's flag prominently displayed, crisscross the globe each day, the day-to-day management of the business is remarkable local in nature. Much of this is due to the massive investments local governments have made in building and maintaining their domestic carriers and aviation infrastructure over the years. Follow the money and you'll ultimately see who is really in control. While there have been calls for years to open up the industry to global competition and allow airlines access to new markets abroad, these moves have been thwarted at nearly every turn. It seems the domestic airline industry is one of the most protected parts of any economy today.

Further, much of the soft landing is *not* attributable to big advances in technology. With the exception of customer relationship management and more fuel-efficient aircraft, technology has not really played the major role many might think in helping the airlines to set the stage for what is coming. Airports, air traffic control systems, and aircraft navigation are not much different than 20 or 30 or even 50 years ago. And significant changes in the near future just aren't going to occur.

So what is it? If neither globalization nor most recent technological progress have prepared the way for the soft landing, then what is making it possible? More than anything else, it is because we have grown our dependency on air travel—and therefore the airlines—over the past decades. Through plain survival, propped up with huge amounts of taxpayer support when needed, the airline industry has become increasingly influential in the lives of more and more people, organizations, and their governments. In other words, access to safe and affordable air travel has become something we couldn't imagine living without, like running water, electricity, or a mobile phone. This rising indispensability finally reached critical mass sometime in the past decade and permitted the airlines to try new things when it comes to managing customer service, operations, and its employees—things that simply weren't possible twenty years ago. It is here that the foundations of the soft landing originate.

Don't think that the industry's leaders saw all of this coming and, then, being smart businesspeople, developed and implemented a successful strategy to get to this moment. Not at all. What has happened since 1992—and I believe 1992 is the tipping point in the industry's evolution—has been a series of attempts (a few successful, but most of them futile) to change the way passengers view the air travel experience. This evolution, coupled with the increasing dependency I just mentioned, made passengers more conducive to accept change. Over the past twenty years, almost imperceptibly, a new model has emerged that gives every indication it will pave the way forward for a more stable industry. I call it Flying Cheap.

The Flying Cheap Strategy, which I'll discuss at length later in the book, provides the airlines with the kind of flexibility they need to better adjust and deal with the inevitable shifts in the landscape. From charging customers extra for almost every imaginable service, to outsourcing entire operations and routes, to using bankruptcy protection to break unions and pay much lower wages, to using the lowest-cost provider for necessities like mainte-nance, the Flying Cheap Strategy has made the airline industry much more efficient than in the past, and, therefore, more elastic. Again, this doesn't mean that everything is smooth sailing ahead and no major crises will occur. Instead, the soft landing, supported by the Flying Cheap Strategy, signifies that the ability of the industry to respond when things get tough will be more responsive and vigorous.

What Does More Stability Mean for Us?

Increased stability underpins greater predictability, which permits us to set more realistic expectations in what we do. The Expectation Gap (the dif-ference between what we expect and what we actually get) can be a tre-mendous source of stress and strain if the gap is too big. An output of the soft landing is that the expectations of an ever-larger number of passengers will be much more realistic than in the past. Today, anyone who expects to be treated like a high-flier had better be sitting in business or first class. For those of us left to tough it out in the back of the plane, we, like any sane person, recognize that the benefits of air travel are no longer found in the means but purely in the ends. Knowing what you're going to get and then getting it, even if it is in cattle class, makes life's difficulties easier to digest.

From a 35,000 feet perspective, a more stable airline industry will make it less difficult to project how much governmental assistance will be needed. In today's fiscally challenging environment, where governments around the world are drowning in huge deficits, the amount available at the public trough will be limited. As governments seek to allocate their scarce re-sources in better ways, a more stable airline industry will help with that cause. Taxpayers should be better served.

But even with the soft landing at hand, this does not mean that the industry and their allies in government still can't screw things up. Looking forward, the specter of aviation security looms as a potential high barrier to any pro-gress. As terrorists and criminals continue to target the global air transport system—as they always have—the way that security is done or not done will go a long way to determining the extent of the soft landing. An overre-action by TSA to the next inevitable spate of attacks could dramatically set things back and cause the kind of deterioration the soft landing is meant to avoid. The possibility that TSA will seriously weaken the industry in order to protect it remains omnipresent. It has nearly happened in recent years and may yet occur when the bad guys once again decide to do something. Other uncontrollable events like a global pandemic or a catastrophic oil spike caused by a major war in the Middle East could make the soft landing much rougher than it should be. And while these could temporarily paralyze the airline industry, the bounce back should be more rapid and stronger due to the soft landing, so long as the leaders of the industry don't go crazy.

Having made the opening argument here, I will go next to the evidentiary portion of my case. The next nine chapters will serve as my attempt to elucidate what I think are the biggest contributors, as well as potential obstacles, to the airline industry's soft landing. The final chapter will serve as my closing argument. At the end, I am confident that I will have effectively made the case that the airline industry is poised for a far better and more stable future than what went before.

The World's Greatest Loss Leader

"A recession is when you have to tighten your belt; depression is when you have no belt to tighten. When you've lost your trousers —you're in the airline business."

—Sir Adam Thomson

Throughout its history, the airline industry has been a "loss leader." Airlines are just like that gallon of milk your local supermarket discounts (in other words, loses money on) to get you through the door to buy other, more profitable stuff. Although there have been periods when airlines actually do make a profit, they are few and far between. To remain in existence, the industry has always relied upon huge amounts of government support. And it always will.

The truth that so many know, but few ever discuss, is that the airline industry would never have developed into the current form without government largesse being there every step of the way. It was government support that spawned air service: first by paying to have planes carry the mail and other cargo; then by funding the expansion of air cargo networks; by building the infrastructure necessary to move passengers, planes, and their cargo safely and efficiently; by underwriting a lot of the costs of manufacturers and developers of new aviation technology; and, of equal importance, keeping the industry flying when times are tough. As you'll see throughout this book, it is most often government—not the industry, nor even the great innovators and pioneers of aviations—that has been the main determinant of how the industry changes, moves forward, or falls back.

Now, before you think this is outrageous and unique, remember that every industry in America, and other countries around the world, feeds in some measure at the public trough. Even before the 2008 financial fiasco, government was solidly in bed with the airlines, farmers, oil companies, mortgage lenders, and dozens of other industries. Today, the banks, automakers, and insurance companies have also come under government funding and greater control.

Lost in the nauseating rhetoric about budget deficits is the fact that the U.S. government spends nearly $1 trillion in the private sector each year. This includes products and services like paperclips, Chevrolets, hotel rooms, the latest version of MS Word, tanks, condoms, airline tickets, and almost anything else you can imagine. (As a point of reference, the total sales at Wal-Mart, the world's largest private company in fiscal year 2011 were a paltry $420 billion). Companies like Boeing and Lockheed Martin always get a big chunk of the national defense budget each year. (One wonders if they could exist at all without government contracts.) But let's not forget that the military was also instrumental in helping start-ups like Oracle (whose first project was subsidized by the CIA) and Hewlett-Packard (whose humble beginnings were rooted in army radar contracts). In fact, the Silicon Valley "miracle" was only possible in the first place because of the huge amount of military spending centered there during World War II, the Korean Conflict, and ever since.[1]

Always at the ready to extract an ever-larger share of government largesse sits the airline industry. Whether it is through direct business with the government (such as transporting U.S. soldiers, bureaucrats, and cargo across the world) or indirect benefits (such as the construction of airports, providing security, air traffic control systems, and so forth), the industry has been

---

[1] A strong analysis of the rise of the Silicon Valley and the linkage between military spending and private enterprise is Bruce Cumings' *Dominion From Sea to Sea* (New Haven, CT: Yale University Press, 2010).

almost completely dependent upon government for its very survival since the inception of air travel. And, if in "free market America" the dependency is so strong, imagine what it's like in the rest of the world, including "socialized Europe and India," and "communist China." Europe's Airbus, Brazil's Embraer, and China's emerging airplane manufacturing sector are each heavily subsidized and supported by the government.

Intensive government involvement with the industry brings with it a huge amount of baggage, including bureaucracy, regulation, Congress, lobbyists, and special interests. Federal, state, and local governments throw billions of dollars in direct and indirect payments to the industry to keep it flying. In exchange, the industry throws back tens of millions—a lot of it, surely, taxpayer dollars—to the same politicians who allocated the original subsidies, in the form of campaign contributions and lobbying efforts. Moreover, there has been rampant waste, fraud, and abuse throughout the history of the government/ industry relationship.

As stated in the opening chapter, I fundamentally believe that the construction and operation of the global air transport system is one of the greatest accomplishments in all of human history, warts and all. If it required huge sums of corporate welfare to make it happen, and more will be needed into the future, so be it. Let's just be honest about it. Let's be mature enough to see clearly the contribution government has made and to identify the areas where waste, fraud, and abuse lie. Then, let's clean it up.

When trying to see where the airline industry is headed, let's not be distracted by such language as "free flight" and "open skies," which suggest an almost *laissez faire* approach to air travel and the industry itself. It's disingenuous. The airline industry needs government—and governments around the world, along with the citizens they represent, need the industry just as much.

Progress has often come from government impetus. Think about the advances that came from building the Panama Canal, harnessing the power of the atom, walking on the Moon, laying the Internet, and developing Global Positioning Systems (GPS). These achievements, and so much more, were possible only because of governmental leadership and money. The airline industry is no exception.

The airline industry has been one of the indispensable catalysts of recent human progress. The ability to be able to move people and cargo via the skies is a vital determinant in how a nation's economy ultimately performs. Aviation supports major sectors of a given economy, including travel and tourism, manufacturing, and logistics. This is the most fundamental reason why governments have underwritten their airline industries. And it makes sense to do so. Just as it makes sense for the grocer to discount that gallon of milk.

Government leaders everywhere know this viscerally. In our "antigovernment" era, it is the rare soul indeed who will compliment the intelligence of our elected officials and bureaucrats. Yet, in this case, some praise is due. It is no coincidence that the richest countries in the world also possess the most advanced aviation sectors. As emerging countries seek to attain "developed market" status, huge investments are being made to upgrade the aviation infrastructures in places like China, India, and Brazil. In the coming decades, governments around the globe will invest trillions of dollars to improve and expand the quality of their airline industries. And this is a good thing for all of us!

But what about all of that "rampant waste, fraud, and abuse"? Aren't these problems that need to be addressed as well? Absolutely. And we will explore a lot of them.

Still, in the end, I remain convinced it is all worthwhile. That, despite the serious shortcomings, the airline industry remains an incredibly valuable asset to the nations and stakeholders it serves. Simply put, the benefits far outweigh the costs. Can it be made better, with more efficiency and less corruption? Certainly. But only if we first understand what is really going on. Let's start by looking at a brief history of the government/industry relationship.

In the Beginning...

Outside of the modest uses of the airplane by the military during World War I, the first experiments of the U.S. Federal Government with airplanes involved the transport of mail. It wasn't until 1918—fifteen years after the Wright Brothers' first flight—when, accepting a suggestion from the National Advisory Committee for Aeronautics (NACA), Congress appropriated $100,000 for the first regularly scheduled airmail service. The route covered 218 miles between Washington, D.C., and New York. In both directions, flights would land at Bustleton Field in Philadelphia for fresh planes and more mail.[2]

This humble, first step by the U.S. Congress put that branch of government at the forefront of the airline industry, where it has remained ever since. It is Congress, more than the President and the Executive Branch, and certainly the airlines, that shapes the future of the industry in America. As it relates to

---

[2] James H. Bruns, *Mail on the Move* (Polo, IL: Transportation Trails, 1992).

the airline industry, Article I, Section 8 of the Constitution gives Congress the ability to regulate the industry—and Congress has done just that.

Initially, the public did not send much mail by air because airmail stamps cost more than stamps for mail sent by train. Congress tried to help by reducing the price of airmail stamps in a few months after the service started—from 24 cents to 16 cents—and eating the loss. And, although usage went up, airmail remained a losing business proposition—and has been so ever since.[3] In the end, it was Congress, in the form of the Post Office—another Article I, Section 8 power—that gave the commercial airlines their true start.[4]

In 1925, Representative Clyde Kelly of Pennsylvania sponsored the Contract Air Mail Act of 1925, commonly referred to as the Kelly Act. This was the first major step toward the hope of creating a private and profitable U.S. airline industry. Using government-subsidized mail transport as the foundation of the new industry, the belief was that this guarantee of revenue would incentivize private sector start-ups to explore carrying passengers along with the mail.[5] After the Kelly Act passed, private companies did, in fact, bid on feeder routes that supplemented the transcontinental air route. The Post Office awarded contracts to private companies, and these companies would later become transportation giants:

- **New York - Boston**—awarded to Juan Trippe, founder of Pan American Airways.
- **Chicago - St. Louis**—awarded to the Robertson Aircraft Corporation with Charles Lindbergh as its chief pilot. Robertson would become part of American Airlines.
- **Elko, Nevada - Pasco, Washington**—awarded to Walter T. Varney, who would later merge with United Air Lines.
- **Salt Lake City - Los Angeles**—awarded to Harris "Pop" Hansue of Western Air.[6]

In 1926, in conjunction with the Kelly Act, President Calvin Coolidge appointed an advisory board to develop a national aviation policy, selecting Dwight Morrow as chairman. Morrow was a senior partner in J.P. Morgan's

---

[3] Ibid.

[4] Roger Bilstein, *Flight in America 1900 –1983: From the Wrights to the Astronauts. Revised Edition* (Baltimore, MD: The John Hopkins University Press, 1994).

[5] Ibid.

[6] Carl Solberg, *Conquest of the Skies, A History of Commercial Aviation in America.* (Boston, MA: Little, Brown and Company, 1979).

bank and later would become the father-in-law of Charles Lindbergh. Morrow counseled that airlines should not be directly subsidized, but rather indirectly supported through federal funding of the construction of a national air transportation system. Congress adopted these recommendations in the Air Commerce Act of 1926, which authorized the Secretary of Commerce to designate air routes, develop air navigation systems, license pilots and aircraft, and investigate accidents. Congress also adopted the board's recommendation for airmail contracting by amending the Kelly Act. With this change, the government began paying carriers according to the weight of the mail. This was potentially a tremendous financial boost to the airlines and it was hoped that it would foster a viable commercial freight industry.[7]

The 1920s also saw advancements in research and training. Harry Guggenheim, a son of the multimillionaire family as well as a former Navy pilot and an aviation enthusiast, established a foundation in the late 1920s to teach aeronautical engineers at mostly private universities and to develop flight instruments. Guggenheim also funded Western Air Express with $180,000 in an experiment to see if airlines could profit from passenger fares alone. Western flew 5,000 passengers from Los Angeles to San Francisco in its first year with a flawless time and safety record. Yet, the company could not make enough money to survive without the government's airmail subsidies. Repeatedly, the dreamers in commercial aviation would invest in ventures that failed. However, when Charles A. Lindbergh made his famous solo flight to Paris in May 1927, his flight set off a Wall Street rush to invest in aviation. His accomplishment fueled the development of commercial aviation. Between 1927 and 1929, investments in aviation stocks tripled.[8]

Unlike today, early commercial passenger airplanes had to fly around mountains, could not fly safely at night, and had to land frequently to refuel. Think you have it tough in economy class? Back then passengers often wore overalls, helmets, and goggles. As somebody once put it, the airplanes were "uninsulated thin sheets of metal, rattling in the wind, and passengers stuck cotton in their ears to stop the noise. Cabins were unpressurized—passengers chewed gum to equalize the air pressure. Fear was rampant."[9]

Nevertheless, despite the discomforts, more and more people were flying. The number of airline passengers in the United States grew from less than 6,000 in 1926 to approximately 173,000 in 1929. Businessmen comprised

---

[7] Bilstein.

[8] Ibid.

[9] Solberg.

most of the passengers, as more and more companies paid for their employees to travel by air.[10] But despite the advances in air travel and the dreams of investors who hoped to get in on the ground floor of a new industry with seemingly unlimited opportunities, airlines that promoted passenger-only routes lost money. Everyone who survived did so because of contracts with the Post Office, which itself was subsidized by the Congress and, ultimately, the American taxpayer.

Regulation

Surprisingly, despite the onslaught of the Great Depression in the 1930s, commercial air travel in America continued to rise. To better manage this burgeoning industry, Congress passed the Civil Aeronautics Act of 1938. That put in place a regulatory body known (after 1940) as the Civil Aeronautics Board (CAB). This act allowed Congress to not only oversee and regulate the air transport industry, but also to promote and foster it.

Those behind the CAB argued that without government oversight, the airlines would concentrate on flying high-volume and high-profit routes, depriving out-of-the-way communities of air transport altogether. Moreover, concentration of airlines on lucrative routes could easily create a business climate of cutthroat competition. In the process, the carriers would undercut the economic stability of the industry and possibly cut corners on safety and maintenance of aircraft in an effort to reduce costs to compete more effectively with the other carriers. Regulation also ensured that no single airline could dominate the market in a particular region and thus be in a position to set high fares because of the lack of competition. Many believed that federal regulation was the best way of assuring that the industry operated efficiently and with the greatest good for the greatest number of Americans, although perhaps at the price of subverting the free market.[11]

Among the CAB's functions, one of the most important was to pick airlines from the available pool for a particular route rather than let the market decide which airline should fly that route. Established carriers already serving a route would usually evaluate new applicants and often found that the applicant lacked some requirement for flying an already-covered route. Thus, new entrants into the business were at a great disadvantage and were often shut out of key routes since the established airlines did not

---

[10] Ibid.

[11] Ibid.

want new competition.[12] Over the next several decades, the CAB was firmly in control of how the airline industry in America operated.

During the same period of time (from the 1930s until the mid-1970s), governments at all levels—federal, state, and local—poured hundreds of billions of dollars into making America's air transport system the largest and most advanced in the world. Most of the airports still used today in the U.S. were built during this period, and the current air traffic control system was developed and staffed with government employees. In addition, the government awarded huge subsidies, underwritten by taxpayers, to airplane manufacturers like Boeing and McDonnell Douglas to assure a steady stream of new planes with new technology. The airline industry's weak balance sheets never affected such decision making.

Deregulation

The existence and power wielded by the CAB created widespread opposition in the country. Opponents of regulation argued that the power of the CAB was anti-American, that it stifled competition and innovation and ultimately cost passengers more money in the form of higher fares.

One major force that helped turn the tide in favor of some deregulation came from abroad. In 1977, Freddie Laker, a British entrepreneur who owned Laker Airways, created the Sky Train service, which offered extraordinarily cheap fares for transatlantic flights. Laker's offerings coincided with a boom in low-cost domestic flights as the CAB eased some limitations on charter flights. These were flights offered by companies that did not actually own planes but leased them from the major airlines. The big air carriers responded by proposing their own lower fares. For example, American Airlines, the country's second largest airline, obtained CAB approval for "SuperSaver" tickets. Each of these events helped to make the case for large-scale deregulation.[13]

The drive to deregulate was further accelerated by none other than President Jimmy Carter, who appointed Cornell University economics professor Alfred Kahn, a vocal supporter of deregulation, to head the CAB. Kahn summed up his thoughts on deregulation this way: "Whenever competition is feasible, it is, for all its imperfections, superior to regulation as a means of serving the public interest." Surprisingly, Kahn, who described himself as "a

---

[12] Ibid.

[13] Howard Banks, *The Rise and Fall of Freddie Laker* (London: Faber & Faber, 1982).

typically liberal Democrat," worked not just for the Democrat Carter, but also closely with Senator Edward Kennedy, the lion of liberalism, who led the battle to have Congress pass the Airline Deregulation Act of 1978.[14] There was stiff opposition to the bill—primarily from the major airlines who feared free competition. They were joined by the labor unions, which feared the entry of lower-paid, non-union employees, and safety advocates, who feared that safety could be compromised.

Public support was, however, strong enough to pass the act. The act kept the major airlines quiet by offering generous subsidies and it appeased airline workers by offering high unemployment benefits if they lost their jobs as a result. The most important effect of the act, whose laws were slowly phased in, was on the passenger market. For the first time in 40 years, airlines could freely enter the market or (from 1981) expand their routes as they saw fit. Airlines (from 1982) also had full freedom to set their fares. In 1984, the CAB was finally abolished since its primary duty—that of regulating the airline industry—was no longer necessary.[15]

While many celebrated deregulation as a triumph of the "free market," it is interesting to note that no one ever seriously suggested that all of the other historic government support for the industry (air traffic control, airports, subsidies to manufacturers and cargo haulers, etc.) be pulled back as well. Those remained fully in place and remain so today.

So, what effect did deregulation have in the short term? First, as expected, many airlines abandoned less profitable routes that took passengers to smaller cities. For example, until 1978, United Airlines had flown to Bakersfield, California, a town of 225,000 people. With deregulation, United pulled out of Bakersfield, depriving the city of any flights, in favor of bigger cities such as San Francisco and Las Vegas.[16]

A second and related effect was the growth of "hub-and-spoke" routes, the foundation of the system we currently have in place today. The major airlines picked key cities as centers for their operations; these key cities served as stops for most flights, even if they were not on a direct route between two other end points. Delta Air Lines had a major hub at Atlanta while Eastern ran its hub operations from Miami. Both airlines ran many daily roundtrip flights from their hubs, thus keeping planes in the air for more

---

[14] *The Guardian*/Richard Adams, "Alfred Kahn Obituary," www.guardian.co.uk/business/2011/jan/12/alfred-kahn-obituary, January 11, 2011, accessed March 19, 2011.

[15] Bilstein.

[16] Ibid.

hours each day and filling more seats. For example, the number of daily nonstop flights between New York and West Palm Beach, Florida, jumped from five to 23.[17]

Third, deregulation allowed new airlines to enter the market without having to agree to the demands of the larger, established airlines. One of these was People's Express, founded by Donald Burr, a shrewd entrepreneur who introduced unconventional methods of management such as low salaries, fewer managers, employees who could perform multiple jobs, and equitable stock ownership by all employees. Burr ran an extremely tight operation in which passengers had to pay for meals on planes and were charged for checked-in baggage. Fares were so low that they were comparable to intercity bus lines. People's Express revenues increased dramatically through the early 1980s, reaching a billion dollars by 1985. Eventually, though, People's couldn't compete with established airlines that also cut their prices but offered significantly better service. The older airlines, being linked with travel agents, also offered the option of advance ticket purchases. Within a year of reaching its peak, in 1986, Burr had to sell People's Express in the wake of rising losses and passenger dissatisfaction.[18]

In general, freed from the rules of the CAB, regional and major airlines inaugurated new routes in droves. Airlines competed in a no holds-barred competition for passenger business. As a result, fares dropped a bit and total operating revenues for the major national and international airlines rose to a high in 1979. The same year was also the peak year for passengers: an unprecedented 317 million passengers flew across American skies.[19] Unfortunately for the airline industry, the 1980s saw high fuel costs, economic recession, and overexpansion in the wake of deregulation each cause serious negative consequences. The airlines recorded a net operating loss of $421 million as early as 1981, when the number of passengers fell to 286 million.[20] Nevertheless, the average airfare dropped by more than 15 percent between 1977 and 1992 (adjusting for inflation). It is estimated that ticket buyers saved as much as $100 billion on fares alone during that period. Deregulation also allowed the proliferation of smaller airlines that took over the shorter routes that were no longer profitable for the big carriers.

---

[17] Solberg.

[18] Ibid.

[19] T. A. Heppenheimer, *Turbulent Skies: The History of Commercial Aviation* (New York, NY: John Wiley & Sons, 1995).

[20] Ibid.

In sum, the major airlines probably suffered the negative consequences of deregulation the most. New smaller airlines and the millions of passengers flying gained the most.[21] Still, the "freedom" given to the airline industry after deregulation did not cut the umbilical to government underwriting and support of the industry. It simply changed the nature of it. As the industry moved through the economic boom of the 1990s, it seemed, even with all of its challenges, that deregulation might have been a good idea from a profitability perspective. Profits for the airlines soared and more and more Americans were flying than ever before. It seemed a corner might finally have been turned. However, the good times wouldn't last. They never do. The industry was still in no position to sustain long-term growth. The economics of the airline industry were not conducive to profits, which has always been the case. Period. Warren Buffett, the famous billionaire investor, summed it up in 1999, when he observed, "As of 1992, in fact . . . the money that had been made since the dawn of aviation by all of this country's airline companies was zero. Absolutely zero."

In a 2008 letter to his shareholders at Berkshire Hathaway, Buffett further articulated, "The worst sort of business is one that grows rapidly, requires significant capital to engender the growth, and then earns little or no money. Think airlines. Here a durable competitive advantage has proven elusive ever since the days of the Wright Brothers. Indeed, if a farsighted capitalist had been present at Kitty Hawk, he would have done his successors a huge favor by shooting Orville down."

Lobbying and the Airline Industry

To overcome the lack of real profits over time, government has had to provide the lifeline. Since its inception, the airline industry has been one of the most potent forces in lobbying for its cause. Whether on Capitol Hill or in state capitals or city halls, the industry and its stakeholders have always sought to make their case known to political decision makers.

Lobbying is as old as democracy itself. While it often gets a bad rap—many times deservedly so—it is a natural input for the democratic process. The origin of the words *lobbying* and *lobbyist* is unclear. The words in the American lexicon seem to have first appeared in a *New Hampshire Sentinel* article in 1820, which quoted George Washington. The article read in part, "Other letters from Washington affirm, that members of the Senate, when the

---

[21] William E. O'Connor, *An Introduction to Airline Economics, Fifth Edition* (Westport, CT: Praeger, 1995).

compromise question was to be taken in the House, were not only 'lobbying about the Representatives' Chamber' but also active in endeavoring to intimidate certain weak representatives by insulting threats to dissolve the Union."[22] A more popular story around the origin of the word *lobbying* involves President Ulysses H. Grant, who would hold court at the Willard Hotel, near to the White House, and meet special interest representatives at the bar in the "lobby."

Whatever the case, neither the creation of the CAB in the 1930s, the expenditure of vast of sums of public money to build the foundation of the air transport system, nor the Deregulation Act of 1978 occurred in a vacuum. Industry lobbyists were there every day, making their case and seeking to influence the budgets of governments across the country. And it hasn't stopped. In 2010, the Air Transport Association, which is the trade group for most of the biggest U.S. airlines, spent $4,470,000 on Capitol Hill alone.[23] This was a bit less than the $4,930,000 in 2009, or the $7,127,000 in 2007.[24] Still, it's a lot of money—and a lot of influence.

Another way of keeping the wheels greased is through the maintenance of the "revolving door." This is an old political scheme where government regulators and airline leaders leave their jobs and take on new ones as lobbyists on behalf of the industry. Already knowing the ins and outs of the industry, as well as who's who, makes any lobbying effort by these insiders incredibly effective.

9/11 and the Great Bailout: A Case Study of the Influence of the Industry[25]

Nearly as shocking as the tragic events of 9/11 was the Bush Administration and Congress' unconditional and unquestioning support of the airline industry following the terrorist attacks. Hours after the World Trade Center towers collapsed, the airline industry's political machine kicked into full gear laying the foundation for a multibillion-dollar plan to bail out the industry. No less than 27 in-house lobbyists along with another group of lobbyists

---

[22] *New Hampshire Sentinel*, April 1, 1820.

[23] Opensecrets.org, www.opensecrets.org/lobby/clientsum.php?lname=Air+Transport+Assn+of+America&year=2010, accessed March 20, 2011.

[24] Ibid.

[25] This case was detailed fully in Andrew R. Thomas' *Aviation Insecurity: The New Challenges of Air Travel* (Amherst, NY: Prometheus Books, 2003).

working for 42 Washington firms, plus the CEOs of several major carriers, went to work right away lining up congressional support for a massive cash infusion of taxpayer money into the industry. "It was masterful," said Sen. Peter Fitzgerald, an Illinois Republican, the lone dissenter in the Senate to federal assistance to the airlines. "The airline industry made a full-court press to convince Congress that giving them billions in taxpayer cash was the only way to save the Republic."[26] It seemed the idea of "Never let a good crisis go to waste" was in full swing.

Part of the army deployed to work back halls and offices to drum up support for a huge bailout plan on Capitol Hill were lobbyists like Linda Daschle, former head of the FAA and wife of Senator Tom Daschle; Haley Barbour, former chairman of the Republican National Committee; and Rebecca Cox, a former Reagan administration official and the wife of U.S. Representative Christopher Cox. (The latter recently oversaw the Security and Exchange Commission, the entity that failed to regulate Wall Street's "innovations" and led the country to the financial collapse of 2008). Leading the charge were several airline CEOs, many of whom were big contributors to the Bush campaign and Congress in the 2000 campaign cycle.

Among them were Donald Carty, CEO of American Airlines, and Gordon Bethune, chief executive of Continental Airlines, both based in Texas and both of whom have known the Bush family for years. "It was the most high-level surgical strike that I have ever seen," said Jeff Munk, a partner at the Washington law firm of Hogan and Hartson and a lobbyist for General Electric, which makes jet engines and leases aircraft. "And the people who made it happen were the CEOs."[27]

In addition to the lobbyist and CEOs holding private meetings on Capitol Hill while fires still raged at the Pentagon and the World Trade Center, several aviation experts were brought in and consulted about what should be done. Daryl Jenkins, director of the Aviation Institute at George Washington University, was one such expert. Jenkins gave Congressional leaders his stamp of approval on the same bailout that was being lobbied for by the industry. The massive cash infusion would be a shot in the arm for the reeling industry, he reasoned, and would send a message to terrorists that America would not allow them to knock out such a vital industry.

---

[26] Seniors USA , "Bailout Showed the Weight of a Mighty and Fast-Acting Lobby," www.senrs.com/airline_bailout_result_of_powerful_lobby.htm, October 10, 2001.

[27] Ibid.

Not surprisingly, in a *USA Today* article a few months later, Jenkins admitted he had been a well-paid consultant for almost every airline and never charged more than the "low six figures" for an annual contract.[28] In the days after September 11, the fleet of experts and consultants on the payroll of the airlines were sought out by many in Congress to substantiate the amount and method of an industry bailout. A senior American Airlines official, who was unnamed, said, "There's a long-standing practice in Washington of supporting people who support you. American has a bunch of consultants charged with going out and building support for issues we support."[29] To Mr. Jenkins's credit, he did not attempt to hide his affiliation with the industry, like many in his profession. When asked about his consulting contracts, he stated, "I'm the only one who won't lie to you."[30]

To further strengthen their case, board members of the six major airlines made personal phone calls to leading members of Congress and the Bush administration. Kirbyjon Caldwell, a Continental director, reportedly phoned three senators, saying the bailout was needed to transform "a moment of fear to a moment of faith." An American Airlines director, John Bachmann, purportedly called Missouri Congressmen Dick Gephardt and Roy Blount to say the industry's losses were nothing less than "breathtaking" and required immediate action.[31]

Eight days after the attacks, with the groundwork laid in place, the CEOs of Delta Airlines, Alaska Airlines, America West Airlines, Federal Express, and Northwest Airlines, along with the CFO for American Airlines were on Capitol Hill in front of the House Committee on Transportation and Infrastructure, seeking immediate financial support from the government. Delta chief Leo Mullin, who served as the spokesman for the group, outlined the needs of the industry.

For most Americans, some degree of taxpayer assistance to the airlines was reasonable; especially since the government-ordered shutdown of all air traffic had cost the industry hundreds of millions of dollars. The only question seemed to be, How much assistance? According to the industry's own analysis and testimony before Congress, the shutdown cost $340 million a day in lost revenue, for a total of $1.36 billion (assuming a four-day as op-

---

[28] Jayne O'Donnell, "Is Support for the American-BA Link up Paid For?" *USA Today,* January 18, 2002.

[29] Ibid.

[30] Ibid.

[31] World Social Web Site/Kate Randall, "How the Airlines Got the $15 Billion Bailout," www.wsws.org/articles/2001/air-08_prn.shtml, October 10, 2001.

posed to a three-day shutdown).[32] This amount seemed legitimate to many. Nevertheless, the airlines eventually got the government to give them billions and billions more over the next months.

The major carriers asked Congress for "an immediate $5 billion cash allocation to address the immediate and devastating impact of September 11 on our industry."[33] In addition, the CEOs asked the government to provide them with access to billions more in loan guarantees. But there was more. The CEOs requested that Congress "pass legislation preserving any existing rights of proper parties to bring claims against the airlines for the experiences and existing deaths of the airlines' passengers."[34] However, such legislation would also stipulate, based on the fact that this was an act of war, "that the airlines would not be liable for the damage to persons and property on the ground." In other words, the airlines would be freed from any legal liability for those who died at the Pentagon, the World Trade Center, or Shanksville, Pennsylvania. In addition, the airlines proposed that Congress expand the war risk insurance program to include domestic operations and assist wherever possible in providing airlines with insurance coverage.

The requests continued. The industry asked Congress to have the federal government take over all the responsibilities and costs associated with aviation security. The airlines asked the government to "provide financial support for all mandated safety requirements, including reinforcement of cockpit doors and enhancement of screening devices," as well as "take over all security screening functions" and the requisite costs associated with it.[35]

To reassure the taxpayers that they wouldn't merely be writing a blank check to the airlines, the industry promised to Congress that it "would fully document each and every claim received from both the cash infusion and the credit facility... under the administration of the Department of Transportation."[36] This was the same Department of Transportation that was charged with overseeing the industry for the past several decades. And, attempting to alleviate any remaining concerns, the airline CEOs insisted that their request was "not a bailout, but rather a package designed solely to re-

---

[32] Testimony of the Air Transport Association on the Financial Condition of the Airline Industry, U.S. House of Representatives Committee on Transportation and Infrastructure, September 19, 2001.

[33] Ibid.

[34] Ibid.

[35] Ibid.

[36] Ibid.

cover the damages associated with the heinous acts of September 11…and offer the public service it is [their] duty to provide."[37]

A mere eleven days after the attacks, President George W. Bush signed into law the Air Transportation Safety and System Stabilization Act. In the House, the vote for the bailout was an overwhelming 356 to 54. In the Senate, the vote went 96 in favor of the bailout and 1—Peter Fitzgerald—against. Bluntly put, the airlines got all they wanted and even more.

Title I of the law earmarked $15 billion to the industry: $5 billion in grants (or, in other words, free money) and $10 billion in secured loans. Other add-ons followed. Title II stated that any increases in insurance premiums charged to the airlines would be reimbursed by the federal government. Title IV dealt with the issue of victim compensation. Spelled out was the manner in which the federal government insured the airlines' against culpability. It offered the 9/11 victims' families $1.6 million each in taxpayer money if they signed a waiver forgoing their right to sue. In Title V, the law guaranteed that federal government would now absorb the responsibility and the cost of aviation security across the United States forever. This freed the airlines from an estimated $1.2 billion in annual security costs and passed the buck to the taxpayers.[38]

Senator Fitzgerald argued that the bailout plan was unfair to workers and unfair to taxpayers. He recognized a strong case existed for compensating the airlines for the temporary government-ordered shutdown of air travel, but "Congress went way beyond this mandate in favor of the airlines, and eventually did write a blank check to the airlines."[39]

Commenting on the airlines' efforts, Representative George Miller, a California Democrat, summed it up when he said, "The big dog got the bone. After September 11, the mood was one of shared sacrifice. People had lost their jobs and their lives. And the first thing that happened was the airline industry came in while everyone else is waiting to see if they can make their mortgage payments."[40]

After the bailout was secured, the industry did pretty much what it wanted to with no strings attached. The carriers sucked up the $5 billion in cash

---

[37] Ibid.

[38] Air Transportation Safety and System Stabilization Act, Public Law 107-42, 49 USC 40101.

[39] Seniors USA , "Bailout Showed the Weight of a Mighty and Fast-Acting Lobby," www.senrs.com/airline_bailout_result_of_powerful_lobby.htm, October 10, 2001.

[40] Ibid.

with no problem. At the same time, almost 100,000 employees were fired, and air transport service was cut off for millions of Americans living in small communities. Meanwhile, costly business ventures continued to be explored and funded by the carriers.

One element that was never brought up during the debate was the fact that the airlines weren't doing very well financially on September 10, 2001. After recovering from a downturn in the early 1990s, caused in part by the first Gulf War and a recession, the airline industry enjoyed its most prosperous period in history. Record profits and an exponential rise in the number of passengers traveling every year gave the airlines the very real impression that high growth could always be assumed. Throughout the mid- to late 1990s, it was not uncommon for a last-minute business traveler to pay $2,000 to fly from Los Angeles to San Francisco or $1,800 to go from Cleveland to Boston. Business was good all across America and the airlines were cashing in.

During 1998 and 1999, the major carriers, believing they were invincible, overextended themselves, buying too many planes and overcharging their best customers, the business travelers. As the dot.com bubble burst in early 2000 and the economy slowed, business travelers—who accounted for as much as 80 percent of airlines' profits—cut back on travel. Companies dramatically reduced the number of times they sent their employees out to do business. Corporate travel departments were now ordered to shop for the lowest fare and book trips far in advance for lower prices. The significant drop in this customer demographic, coupled with higher fuel prices throughout the first half of 2001, threatened airline profitability and pushed some companies to the verge of bankruptcy well before the September 11 attacks.

Robert Crandall, former CEO of American, commented on the problems of the airlines prior to the attacks when he observed, "I'm not sure 9/11 by itself had any particularly profound impact [on the industry]. But it exacerbated the problems they had before 9/11."[41] Duane Woerth, president of the Air Line Pilots Association, was among many who saw the economics of air travel fundamentally changing before 9/11. "When the stock market popped, the airlines held onto this pricing model where they tried to make all their money off 20 percent of the travelers."[42]

---

[41] Hoovers Online, "Airlines don't see relief over the horizon," www.hoovers.com /fp.asp?la..._id=nr200209071180.3_2b4e0042b6ecefe72, September 7, 2002.

[42] Ibid.

A September 19, 2001, editorial in the *Wall Street Journal* blasted the idea of the bailout, stating: "Other industries are now suffering through the same devastating aftermath of the terrorist attack. Insurance companies are facing costs that could total $20 to $30 billion. After airlines get their money, what's to stop politicians from tapping taxpayers to bail out every other industry?"

The industry did nothing to obscure the fact that despite the multibillion-dollar bailout, tens of thousands of airline employees would be fired. Nearly every major carrier fired at least 20 percent of its staff, with United Airlines and American Airlines both cutting 20,000 jobs. US Airways fired the biggest percentage of its workforce, 23 percent, and laid off 11,000 workers. Delta and Continental fired 13,000 and 12,000 employees, respectively, after receiving the bailout funds.[43]

A few days after the taxpayers' money started flowing from the U.S. Treasury, the parent company of United Airlines made a down payment on 30 brand-new luxury business jets. The purchase was part of a new strategy that United had embarked on to sell shares of aircrafts to corporations, celebrities, and other wealthy individuals. Representative Peter DeFazio, an Oregon Democrat, remarked on the purchase, "It's outrageous. On one hand, they say they need an immediate cash infusion from the government, no strings attached, and on the other they are wiring money to France."[44]

Notwithstanding the fact that Section 105 of the new law instructed the secretary of the DOT "to ensure that all communities that had scheduled air service before September 11, 2001, continue to receive adequate air transportation," service was immediately cut to dozens of cities around the country by the airlines. Several members of the House and Senate who days before had supported the airline bailout found themselves at loggerheads with the same industry that was now cutting air service to their constituents.

By the end of October 2001, 25 Congressional members petitioned the department of transportation to step in to prevent elimination of the air routes that were supposedly protected by the same legislation they had passed five weeks earlier.

It goes without saying that the actions by the airlines immediately after they secured the assistance of the U.S. taxpayers were not in agreement with

---

[43] BBC Business News, "Aviation Job Losses Reach 400,000," www.news.bbc.uk, January 11, 2002.

[44] Free-market.net, J.D. Tuccille, "The Baneful Bailout," www.free-market.net/spotlight /bailout/. No longer available.

what President Bush publically announced when he asked for the bailout 11 days after the 9/11 attacks. The President and Congress assured all Americans that the legislation would provide urgently needed tools to assure the stability of the nation's commercial airline system.

Beyond the billions directly transferred from the pockets of taxpayers to the coffers of the airlines as a result of the bailout, the industry received billions more in tax refunds through an engineered loophole in an economic stimulus bill signed by the President in March 2002. Under a previous law, airlines could use only losses from one year to offset tax obligations in the previous two years. However, under the new law, businesses—including the airlines—were able to extend their losses over a five-year period. In this case, it included the years 1996–2000, the industry's most profitable period in history. Estimates placed the refunds for some of the major carriers at about $464 million for United and around $200 million each for U.S. Airways, American, and Delta.[45] It makes one wonder if the bailout of the airline industry after 9/11 was a prelude and template for the bailouts in the fall of 2008 after Lehman Brothers melted down.

Fast-forward to today. The airline industry is still losing billions money. It has just gone through the worst financial period in its history. So, whom does the Air Transport Association bring in to head the industry's largest trade group? Nicholas E. Calio, a former official in both Bush administrations who had previously led lobbying operations for Citigroup. Under his watch, the banking giant received billions in federal bailout funds after the 2008 financial crash.[46] In just two years, despite tremendous losses, the ATA was able to find more than $8 million to spend on lobbying the Obama administration. Certainly Mr. Calio was brought on to make sure that was money was well spent.

While government is *the* major player in determining where the industry is going, it is not the only factor. Suffice it to say, I could spend the rest of this book illustrating the deals that go on between the airlines and government. We will look at many of them in the chapters that follow; but that's not our major purpose here. We want to end up with a clear view of where the industry is headed. And government clearly matters.

---

[45] Dan Reed, "Airlines to Get Millions in Refunds After Bailout," *Knight-Ridder News Service,* March 7, 2002.

[46] Washington Post/Dan Eggers, "Airline lobbying group to hire Nicholas Calio," www.washingtonpost.com/wp-dyn/content/article/2010/11/29/AR2010112903951_Comments.html, November 29, 2010.

The Airline Industry and the Globalization Paradox

"It has been said that arguing against globalization is like arguing against the laws of gravity. "

—Kofi Annan

When it comes to globalization, the airline industry is wrapped in a paradox. For those who view the industry primarily from a passenger seat, the industry is one of the great drivers of globalization. The airline industry, despite all of the trials and tribulations associated with modern day travel, *undoubtedly* makes it easy to cross national boundaries; it reduces the time for traveling; it brings the opportunity to connect to human beings in all corners of the world; and it does so at relatively low prices to the flying public. Yet, despite these truths, the industry itself remains remarkably local in its focus and approach—and has been so since its inception. As you saw in Chapter 2, governments around the world, led by the United States, have been remarkably consistent in defending and supporting their nation's "loss leaders," often enduring tremendous financial burdens.

Presently: Semi-Globalization

At the beginning of each semester, I ask the students in both my graduate and undergraduate international business classes a pretty simple question: What is the most important determinant of how a company operates? After more than eight years, the answers have tended to be about the same: the free market, the law of supply and demand, customer needs, and, probably because the subject matter is international business, globalization. While each of these answers touch on elements that can influence how a company delivers its products and services, they miss the most important players that shape the conduct of business and the performance of the marketplace: national and local government. It is government that makes the rules of how companies must operate. Government sets the parameters. It is the force behind taxes, price controls, subsidies, regulations, intellectual property, and so much more. Companies can try to influence how government controls the marketplace through lobbying and the political process. At the end, though, the *laissez faire* of Adam Smith is merely an ideal—and it always will be.

This is not to indict my students or the school where I teach. The University of Akron's business school is fully accredited and regularly ranked by *Business Week* and the *Princeton Review* as one of the top schools in the world. Instead, what this lack of understanding from my students reveals, I think, is a shortage of knowledge about government and the huge impact it has over the private sector. And, also, a complete misunderstanding about what globalization is—and isn't.

This shouldn't be a surprise, as my students are products of a time where government came to be marginalized in favor of the "free market." The conventional wisdom for these young folks as they came of age held that the world was "flattening" and that government couldn't do anything nearly as well as the private sector.

The underpinnings of this anti-government strain came from Milton Friedman and his colleagues in the Chicago School of Economics. The financial crisis of the early and mid-1970s gave way to their viewpoint that anything that could reduce governmental influence over the market was a good thing. The high-inflation, high-unemployment conditions that existed at the time were precisely because the markets hadn't been freed and unleashed from governmental constraints. Hence, the deregulation of the airlines and, later, mortgage lending and financial derivatives. In the era of Reagan and beyond, seemingly anything that blocked the free market from expanding was viewed as anti-American and anti-capitalist. Government was *the* problem—*the* impediment to entrepreneurs, risk takers, and those who create the "real value" for society.

Further, my students were told from many of their political leaders that the expansion of free markets is a net-positive and the benefits for them would be fantastic: that theirs will be the first truly global generation, both in spirit and practice. Because of globalization, companies will achieve economies of scale, greater efficiencies, and be able to leverage resources anywhere. Regional trade agreements like NAFTA and international "non-governmental" bodies like the World Trade Organization—both brought to the forefront under President Clinton, a Democrat—are also good for us. All of this will inexorably and forever alter the way things are done, finally getting government out of the way and allowing the free market to consistently improve the quality of our lives. In nearly every business conversation or classroom, the topic of globalization comes up. Everyone, it seems now, takes globalization to be a *fait accompli*. We assume that customers, supply chains, marketing campaigns, managers, and workers are all becoming increasingly globalized.

This thinking is further reinforced by influential media hacks like Thomas Friedman, whose *The World Is Flat* is one of the bestselling books ever on the subject of globalization. With the credibility only a *New York Times* columnist can possess, Friedman argues simply and naively that barriers are falling down and obstacles like national borders, laws, and customs are being replaced with a "flat world." In it, outdated things like governments and local institutions are being wiped out and replaced by global companies, brands, and ideas. *The World is Flat* is one of the most recommended freshman reading requirement at colleges and universities across America. Interestingly, the 450-plus pages that lay out Friedman's thesis don't contain a single table, chart, or footnote to back up its pronouncements.[1]

Like the vacuous *The World in Flat*, the YouTube sensation "Shift Happens" is a staple of high school and college classrooms. It speaks about the seemingly

---

[1] Pankaj Ghemawat, *World 3.0: Global Prosperity and How to Achieve It* (Cambridge, MA: Harvard Business Review Press, 2011), p. 34.

unstoppable rise of China and India and how they are already challenging American supremacy in innovation. My son, who recently graduated from our relatively prosperous suburban high school district, was shown the video six times in his four years there. As of early 2011, it had nearly six million views on YouTube.[2]

Created by Karl Fisch, a high-school teacher, the presentation throws out some wild statistics, including that there are more honors students in India and China than the entire youth population of North America. Moreover, if every single job in North America was shipped to China, there would still be a labor surplus in China.[3] While this all sounds impressive, it simply is not accurate. What this incredibly influential "piece of research" fails to mention is that, according to the People's Bank of China, for example, sixty million Chinese—a population equivalent to that of a large European country—live in a middle-class household (those earning more than $20,000 a year). While of the remaining people in China, six hundred million live in households earning less than $3 a day and another 440 million Chinese live in households earning between $3 and $6 a day. This means that 80 percent of China lives in conditions that compare with the poverty of sub-Saharan Africa.[4] It also forgets to mention that the illiteracy rate in India, according to the World Bank, is over 50 percent.[5] And, that much of the research being produced by these burgeoning "honors students" is riddled with plagiarism.

My point here is that we have a large segment of our population who believes, wrongly, that globalization is in constant expansion and therefore should be embraced wholeheartedly. Globalization—and its role in our lives—is more nuanced than the broad generalities that are often passed off as undeniable truths.

The airline industry is much more reflective of the semi-global nature of things than the unabashedly "all in" type of globalization that has been propagated over the last thirty years. The airline industry, like so much of the rest of humanity, is predominantly local. In the U.S., which has the largest single air transport network in the world, there were 629 million domestic passenger trips versus 88 million international departures and arrivals in 2010, as shown in Table 3-1.

---

[2] http://www.youtube.com/watch?v=ljbI-363A2Q.

[3] Ibid.

[4] George Friedman, *The Next Decade: Where We've Been...And Where We're Going* (New York: Doubleday, 2011).

[5] World Bank: India Data and Statistics 2011, www.worldbank.org.in/WBSITE/EXTERNAL/COUNTRIES/SOUTHASIAEXT/INDIAEXTN/0,,menuPK:295609~pagePK:141132~piPK:141109~theSitePK:295584,00.html.

Table 3-1. Passenger Trips: Domestic vs. International Destinations, 2002-2010, All U.S. Carriers. Source: Bureau of Transportation Statistics T-100 Market data.

U.S. Airline Passenger Distribution	2002	2004	2006	2008	2010
Domestic	551,960,680	629,768,486	658,362,617	651,709,940	629,517,348
International	60,878,039	70,462,241	82,735,582	88,750,960	88,206,634

This jives with numbers on other seemingly "highly globalized" activities: only 20 percent of all the stocks in the world are owned by foreign investors; less than 18 percent of all Internet traffic is routed across national borders; less than 2 percent of all telephones calls are to or from people outside our own country; and it is estimated that about 90 percent of all of the world's people alive today will never venture outside the country in which they were born.[6]

What about all the new technology of today, including Skype, Facebook, and Twitter? Aren't they making globalization even more inevitable? Maybe we should look back to George Orwell, who, in 1944 as the telephone, computer, and transatlantic flights had taken hold, wrote about technology shrinking the world: "Reading recently a batch of rather shallowly optimistic 'progressive' books, I was struck by the automatic way people go on repeating certain phrases which were fashionable before 1914. Two great favorites are the 'abolition of distance' and the 'disappearance of frontiers.' "[7] As Mark Twain said, "When you find yourself in the majority, pause and reflect." At its core, globalization's proponents are really about getting as many government and industry controls in order to have a worldwide free market as possible. This flies in the face of the way the airline industry has historically operated.

Dealing with the International Component

As early as 1910, as airplanes began to crisscross the skies—and borders—of Europe, a meeting was held in Paris. Representatives from the major powers sat down and hoped to hash out what this new technology might

[6] Pankaj Ghemawat, *World 3.0: Global Prosperity and How to Achieve It* (Cambridge, MA: Harvard Business Review Press, 2011), p. 35- 40.

[7] George Orwell, "As I Please," *Tribune,* May 12, 1944.

mean—and how they could regulate it. As with so many other issues going on in Europe at the time, no one could agree. Ironically, the first bilateral agreement was signed in July 1913 between France and Germany, which allowed for airships from Germany to enter French airspace and remain in France.[8] Tragically, World War I would start a little more than a year later.

Nine years later, after the bloodletting of the War to End All Wars, the Europeans, now in an apparently more conciliatory mode, sat down once again in Paris to figure out how the airline industry should be managed. This time a transnational organization—made up primarily of lawyers and bureaucrats—was created to deal with the legal questions posed by cross-border air traffic: the International Commission for Air Navigation. It was decided that the Commission would meet once a year to go over any technical changes and developments.[9]

Around the same time, across the Atlantic, the nations of the Western Hemisphere were going through similar machinations. Nothing much was done, however. Finally, in 1928, a Pan-American meeting was held in Havana to deal with the rise of international flights. A lot of conversations—and an equal amount of rum—were certainly tossed about. Still, no agreements were reached about how to handle international air traffic in the Americas. In fact, except for Europe's Commission, most nations across the globe remained very strict about allowing planes to fly nonstop over their territory until the onset of World War II.[10]

The war was a game changer for aviation. Rapid advances in aircraft technology and designs compelled governments to look differently at the future of aviation. The development of the airplane into a mainstream form of transportation—now a peer with the train, automobile, and truck—raised several critical questions: How would airports be constituted? What language, if any, would be the lingua franca? How would weather-reporting systems operate? What about safety, security, and maintenance standards? What about the arrangements for how an airliner would fly from one country to another or over a third country?[11] As the war began to wind down and the Allies started planning for peace, it became clear that answers were needed.

---

[8] "Exchange of Notes Between France and Germany Concerning Aerial Navigation," signed at Berlin, July 26, 1913. A copy can be found in the *American Journal of International Law*, Vol. 8, No. 3, July 1914.

[9] Gary Elphinstone, "The Early History of Aviation Security Practice" in *Aviation Security Management: Volume 1*, edited by Andrew R. Thomas, (Praeger Security International, Westport, CT), p. 6.

[10] Ibid.

[11] Ibid.

The United States was far and away the global leader in the aviation sector, as it still is today. During World War II, U.S. dominance was unprecedented. America manufactured the vast majority of all aircraft, both military and civilian. As the post-war world started coming into focus, it was clear that aviation, and America's mastery of it, would play a key role in the future. To that end, in September 1944, the U.S. invited representatives from 55 nations to a conference in Chicago. The Chicago Convention on International Civil Aviation, as it came to be called, sought to hammer out what the future of air travel and flight would look like. For five weeks, the delegates considered the challenges and made recommendations. Those recommendations would later be formalized into the first set of truly international rules governing how the airline industry would operate.

To this end, the International Civil Aviation Organization (ICAO), an agency of the United Nations, was established in 1948. It advertises itself as "the global forum for cooperation among its Member States and with the world aviation community. ICAO sets standards and recommended practices for the safe and orderly development of international civil aviation. In its ongoing mission to foster a global civil aviation system that consistently and uniformly operates at peak efficiency and provides optimum safety, security and sustainability."[12] To its credit, ICAO has made tremendous strides in standardizing across borders critical aviation functions like air traffic control, weather reporting, safety, and security. Nevertheless, it has been unable to force individual countries to forgo their national interest and open up their borders. As Winston Churchill observed, "All nations have interests"—and nations have fought tooth and nail from the beginning to protect their domestic airline industry from foreigners.

The last time the airline industry experienced a big "global moment" was when the U.S. deregulated in 1978. Prior to that, only four U.S. carriers—Pan American (PanAm), Trans World Airlines (TWA), Northwest, and Braniff—had authority to fly overseas. Departure points for overseas flights were Kennedy Airport in New York for transatlantic destinations, Los Angeles or San Francisco for transpacific flights, and Miami for Latin American flights. Immediately after deregulation, several more U.S. carriers—American, United, Delta, and, for a time, Eastern—obtained clearance and acquired some international routes.

As the case for "market forces" gained steam, both in the U.S. and abroad, the deregulation of the domestic industry in the U.S. was copied to varying degrees in much of the rest of the world. It has given us the airline industry

---

[12] ICAO Strategic Objectives, www.icao.int.

in the current form. Increased competition has, at least in domestic markets, spurred innovations like the hub-and-spoke routing systems and new low-cost carriers such as Southwest Airlines in the U.S. and easyjet and Ryanair in Europe.[13] While this has led to more planes from more carriers—and nations—traversing the world's skies, those planes are often only allowed to make one stop and take-off in the foreign country.

Protectionism Is the Rule

Why do governments so staunchly defend their domestic airline industries? To say it is only because of a fear of competition from abroad would be overly simplistic. Much of the closed nature of the airline industry is really about politics; and, as Former Speaker of the House Tip O'Neil observed, "All politics is local." Minimizing competition keeps those who run governments in control. It keeps their hands in the mix. While domestic flights have become increasingly deregulated, the infrastructure that supports the industry remains firmly government-run and, most often, government-owned. Unrestricted globalization threatens this.

One of the more stunning examples of politicians using the aviation infrastructure for their own personal gain is the John Murtha Johnstown-Cambria County Airport, two hours east of Pittsburgh. Named after the late Democratic Congressman from Johnstown, the gleaming airport is a testament to the largesse and corruption regularly found in domestic aviation programs. On an regular weekday, an average of four passengers line up to board a flight, outnumbered by seven security staff members and supervisors, all suited up in gloves and uniforms to screen six pieces of luggage. For three hours a day, no commercial or private planes take off or land. Three commercial flights leave the airport on weekdays, all bound for Dulles International Airport.[14]

The key to the airport's world-class facilities—and, indeed, its continued existence—was $200 million in federal funds in the past decade and the powerful patron who steered most of that money here. Congressman Murtha is credited with securing at least $150 million for the airport.[15] The lawmaker, who used the airport frequently during his campaigns, steadily steered

---

[13] "The Misery of Flying," *The Economist*, January 8, 2011, p. 67.

[14] Carol Leonnig, "Murtha's Earmarks Keep Airport Aloft: State-of-the-Art Pennsylvania Facility Sees Few Travelers but Lots of Funding," *Washington Post*, April 19, 2009.

[15] Ibid.

millions of taxpayer dollars to it to build a new terminal with a restaurant; a long, concrete runway sturdy enough to handle large jets; and a high-tech radar system usually reserved for international airports. Murtha, who headed the House Appropriations defense subcommittee, fought for airport funding as a way to bring jobs to his congressional district, devastated by losses in the steel and coal industries.[16] Still, each of the six daily flights that the United Express local carrier makes to and from the airport is subsidized, costing taxpayers about $1.4 million, or $147 per passenger, last year.

In addition to the passenger subsidy, the airport property is dotted with big-ticket items and buildings funded with Murtha's help. An $8 million radar system for detecting weather problems more than 100 miles away spins on the southern edge of the property. Murtha had said that the system would create at least a dozen air traffic control jobs, but the state Air National Guard, which was supposed to staff it, said personnel reductions have left the radar unmanned. A $17.8 million earmark in 2006 from the Defense Department replaced the airport's 7,000-foot-long asphalt runway with a reinforced concrete bed capable of handling larger civilian and military jets, but it is not being employed for that purpose. A $6.5 million, three-story National Guard and Reserve training center, resembling a rustic ski lodge, is perched on Airport Road. A new air traffic control tower was built in 1999 for $6.8 million, after Murtha persuaded Congress to add the project to the federal budget. He also got the funds that year to build the new terminal, where his portrait graces the entrance. In 1998, at Murtha's urging, the Marine Corps agreed to move a helicopter unit to Johnstown and constructed a $14 million hangar and training facility at the airport's southeastern edge.

And there's more. In 2007, the airport authority fired longtime manager Joe McKelvey after he used FAA funds to buy a Chevrolet Tahoe SUV to use at the airport. The FAA had initially approved the expense for a safety vehicle on the property, but other agency managers later questioned it. The same day, over objections from members of the airport's board, the authority hired MTT Aviation Services. The company is a subsidiary of Mountaintop Technologies, a defense contractor that had received at least $23 million in earmarks from Murtha since 2001 and is run by his close friend. The subsidiary was formed to handle fuel sales and other services at the airport shortly before its role was expanded to airport manager. MTT hired a lobbying firm that had one of Murtha's former staffers as a lead lobbyist and had once employed Murtha's brother.[17] In the European Union, there is a

---

[16] Ibid.

[17] Ibid.

move afoot to implement what is called the Single Sky plan. Although the EU purports to be a model of economic integration, and it is many ways, this is not the case when it comes to the airline industry. New technologies in the form of the next generation of air traffic control system have been blocked for years because it is feared that implementation will ultimately reduce the number of people needed to operate the system in each country, which will weaken the influence of the unions and the politicians they support.

The situation in Spain may be the most illustrative. For years, the Spanish government reduced the salaries and training of its air traffic controllers. Many people stayed away from the profession, which ultimately lead to a dramatic shortage of controllers, whose ranks had been further cut by retirements and attrition. This allowed the remaining controllers to negotiate huge pay increases and benefit packages. Government leaders, who feared crippling strikes if they didn't give in, acquiesced. By 2005, only two-thirds of Spanish controllers' annual hours were on standard salary. The rest was overtime, paid at triple-time rates. In 2009, some controllers earned more than $1 million. Early retirement was allowed at age 52.[18] When governments tried to push back, the Spanish controllers and their fellow travelers in France, Italy, Belgium, and Greece staged walkouts, cancelling thousands of flights and delaying thousands more.

Even security gets politicized. Politicians will knowingly support stupid and wasteful measures with the expectation that this "attention to detail" will keep them from getting blamed if something happens.

Isn't Anti-Globalization Self-Defeating?

Although nationalistic politics have battled against serious cross-border activity- and won most of the battles, the forces of globalization are unlikely to allow preservation of the status quo forever. Commercial aviation, like most mature (some would argue declining) industries in America and Europe, is witnessing a paradigm shift: developed-nation consumers will no longer be the primary driver of global consumption. While Western airlines and their supporters seek to maintain their grip on their markets at home, emerging market consumers are increasingly anxious to book their first trip outside of a sovereign national border that for too long has represented a limitation to mobility.

---

[18] Daniel Michaels, "Sky Wars: Europe Battles to Erase Borders in the Air," *Wall Street Journal*, May 4, 2011 p. A14.

Today's high-growth emerging market economies are home to a vast and burgeoning middle-class consumer segment that has largely gone either unserved or under-served by most prominent industries, including commercial aviation. While Western consumers fret over baggage fees and in-flight access to more than one bag of peanuts, tomorrow's Chinese passenger fantasizes about a 7,015 mile (11,309 km) trip from Beijing to Boston, USA: a ten-day excursion that, booked only seven days out through Expedia, will cost a total of $1,783.50 US Dollars (11,723.12 Chinese Yuan) per person, including four star accommodations at Boston's famed Omni Parker Hotel and a rental car for the duration of the stay.

Going forward, the industry is going to have to deal with legions of new customers from places like China and India who will come to take flying for granted. Given their rich international experience, you might think the major Western airlines—the so-called legacy carriers like Delta Air Lines, British Airways, and Air France, among many others—would be well positioned to take advantage of globalization, now that other industries have caught up to them in seeing the profitability possibilities of worldwide commerce. But that's not the case; in fact, unlike for virtually every other industry, for the traditional airlines, globalization is not an opportunity but one of the gravest threats.

The Present

Phileas Fogg had won his wager, and had made his journey around the world in eighty days . . . The eccentric gentleman had thoroughly displayed all of his marvelous qualities of coolness and exactitude. But what then? What had he really gained by all this trouble? What had he brought back from this long and weary journey?

Nothing, say you? Perhaps so; nothing but a charming woman, who, strange as it may appear, made him the happiest of men!

Truly, would you not for less than that make the tour around the world?

—From Jules Verne's *Around the World in Eighty Days*

Flying Cheap, Part 1

Passengers

"The fewer expectations you have, the better."

—Laurie Anderson

I was raised in a very comfortable middle-class American home that took the big family vacation every summer. Except for once, we always drove. It may seem a bit strange that all of these years later I still vividly remember the time we flew from Cleveland, Ohio, to Charleston, South Carolina, to stay at a rented home on Edisto Beach. But for those of us old enough to remember, air travel used to be something that was reserved only for very special occasions or businesspeople. Flying anywhere was damn expensive and the old family truckster remained a far better option for most families.

I remember several times hearing friends of my parents boast about their upcoming vacation and how it involved a flight to so and so destination. They would wait for someone to ask a detail about their flight: maybe which airline or connecting city they would travel through. Inevitably, someone *would* ask and the soon-to-be-travelers would start spouting all the specifics about their itineraries. My sisters and I would listen in envious silence.

If you grew up in the 1970s or before, you can likely remember conversations in which people bragged about how much they paid for something. To have paid more for a product or service indicated that a higher-quality item had been purchased. Not so today. For the last twenty-plus years, bragging rights have gone to the person who got a good price, a fabulous discount, a great deal. This is true with airline tickets as well. Price sensitivity—resulting from discounting, sales, or everyday low prices—has become the norm in much of America and around the world.

Because of the availability of cheaper flights to more places than ever before, air travel has become a real possibility for billions of people around the world. And, because of this, flying has moved from being the exclusive territory of the "jet set" to a true form of public transportation. The openness and affordability of air travel has brought the public with all of its baggage—in every sense of the word—to the once hallowed halls of the world's airports.

Let's be honest; when walking through a terminal or sitting on a plane, one immediately gets the impression that he or she is merely part of the masses. Like going to the mall or driving on the freeway, air travel has brought all of the elements of society closer together. Unfortunately, some of those elements are not the best intentioned, brightest, or most considerate.

So when did all of this change? When did air travel go from being a high-end, Tiffany's type of experience to the cattle class, Wal-Mart like encounter it is today? We can trace it back to the summer of 1992—14 years after the airline industry deregulated in the United States.

Ticket Prices After Deregulation and Before 1992

The promised benefits to travelers from the deregulation of the airlines in the form of lower ticket prices never really materialized until 1992. The belief was that less government and more market forces would lead to increased competition, and, therefore, lower fares for passengers. Actually, the period between 1978 and 1991 did see some fares fall, but the overall savings on tickets from the major carriers were pretty marginal.[1] The reason was that the big airlines were able to separate themselves from each other through the expansion of their own hub-and-spoke systems and, therefore, keep prices relatively high.

---

[1] Steven A. Morrison and Winston Clifford, *The Economic Effects of Airline Deregulation* (Washington, D.C.: Brookings Institution, 1986).

The creation of hub-and-spoke systems in the airline system originated in the 1950s when Delta set up its hub in Atlanta. Federal Express built up Memphis as its hub in the 1970s. The idea behind a hub-and-spoke system is simple: bring disparate passengers, planes, and cargo to one centralized location where they can then be efficiently re-routed to their final destinations. After deregulation, every major carrier set out to build their own hub-and-spoke system. From an airline's point of view, this made good sense; not so much from the passenger's.

Governments, especially state and local entities, have historically been big supporters of the hub-and-spoke system. Having a hub in your state, county, or city means a lot of jobs, investment, federal government support, and prestige. Politicians fall over each other trying to attract new hubs and keep their existing ones. Huge subsidies, promises of airport improvements, and big tax breaks are dangled all over the country in the hopes that one of the major carriers will bite. Bidding wars are common and the airlines are happy to play one city off another to get the best deal.

Until the early 1990s, the hub-and-spoke system kept competition to a minimum and therefore restricted the cost of tickets. If you wanted to fly from Toledo to Orlando, you would have to fly first through a hub in Chicago or Cleveland controlled by United or Continental. Then you would be routed to Orlando. This ability to funnel passengers through their hubs ensured the carriers a high degree of control over the prices they charged. In a kind of gentleman's agreement, the major carriers were sure not to tread too much on each other's hubs.

The real growth of passengers in the 1980s came in large part from low-cost upstarts like Southwest. This model provided the kinds of cheap tickets that millions of new passengers needed in order to access the benefits of air travel. The entrance into the market of low-cost carriers was one of the principal benefits of deregulation.

Throughout the 1980s, the majors, which were still carrying the vast majority of passengers in America, fought tooth-and-nail to differentiate themselves from the rising budget-carriers. Frequent flyer programs were introduced, with American being the first major to do so in 1981. Television advertisements throughout the decade continued to reinforce the view that air travel was an exclusive experience, reserved for gentlemen and ladies. Flight crews were depicted as young and beautiful, happy to serve. Passengers were portrayed as well dressed and rich. Champagne glasses were prominently displayed. It's no accident that George Gershwin's classic "Rhapsody in Blue" was the signature theme for United, which asked customers to come fly the "friendly skies" with them.

Additional pressure on the majors also came from the rising costs incurred by the expansion of their hub-and-spoke networks. Three majors—Pan Am, Eastern, and Continental—went bankrupt, leaving only three big players unscathed by 1990: American, United, and Delta. However, the reduction of the number of majors and the increase in new passengers didn't translate into profits for the industry during the 1980s. Losses were substantial. Nevertheless, it seemed by the end of the decade that the industry had finally turned a corner and the good times were not far off. A seemingly sustainable business model for the industry was emerging: the majors would serve the higher-end category of passengers through their hub-and spokes and the budget carriers would meet the needs of the new, price-sensitive fliers.

Recession, Desert Storm, and the Summer of '92

Any optimism about the industry quickly faded when the armies of Saddam Hussein invaded oil-rich Kuwait on August 2, 1990. Oil prices surged upwards almost overnight by around 10%, which quickly lead to a comparable rise in airline fares as fuel costs rose. At the same time, America and most of the developed economies around the world were going through some rough times. Japan, the world's second largest economy, began to melt down earlier in the year, and America and Europe were also slowing down. This combination of rising fares and worsening economic prospects hit the industry square in the face. The blow to the airlines was further exacerbated by security fears that the looming war with Iraq might lead to terrorist attacks against the air transport system. Travelers stayed away in droves. The result was that 1990 and 1991 were two of the worst years in the history of commercial aviation. Estimates held that the losses of the industry from 1988–1992 ($10 billion) were more than the total profits the industry had earned since its inception.

As 1991 became 1992, the industry faced an even worse year. A global recession was firmly in place and prospects for a turnaround were bleak. The summer travel season looked like it was going to be the worst one in living memory. The airlines were regularly cancelling flights because of a lack of passengers. Greater losses were mounting. Something needed to be done.

On May 28, the mother of all fare wars broke out. Northwest introduced its "Grownups Fly Free" promotion where one adult would travel free with any child aged 2 to 17. American answered immediately with fare reductions of up to 50% under the guise of its new "Value Pricing." Delta did the same thing. It became "the sale of the century," as then American-CEO Robert Crandall put it.[2] Fares dropped all over the country, and a bloodbath ensued as the airlines undercut each other in a race to the bottom. Almost overnight, flights for the rest of the summer were filled beyond capacity.

Three days into the fare war, Hertz Corporation bought 20,000 new cars to meet demand for rentals. It also held on to 10,000 vehicles scheduled to go out of service. Hertz, which was 49%-owned by Ford Motor Co., also went so far as to buy General Motors cars to fill the gaps in its fleet. "Frankly, we took whatever we could get, from anywhere," explained Craig R. Koch, a Hertz executive vice-president.[3]

For those working for any airline at that time, the Summer of '92 was utter madness. New travelers, completely unfamiliar with the rites and rituals of air travel, flooded into terminals and onto planes. According to one manager in Atlanta, the checked-luggage of choice for passengers there was a Hefty trash bag. Eighteen-hour workdays were the norm. Flights were overbooked, delays far too common, complaints irrational. Confusion reigned. In September, when things finally returned to a semblance of order, American employees at Chicago's O'Hare had t-shirts printed up that read "I Survived the Summer of '92." They were worn publically for about a week before management quietly asked them to cover up.

Air Travel Becomes a Commodity

While nobody realized it at the time, the dramatic slashing of fares by the majors in the Summer of '92 was a game-changing moment for the airline industry. It's not a stretch to say that the era of Flying Cheap was inaugurated at that moment. And the last 20 years have seen the evolution—or devolution, depending on your point of view—of a new business model: one that is based on increasingly low prices and outsourcing. While the majors tried to reinstitute higher fares—and were in fact successful at doing so a few times over the past two decades—fares were lower in 2011 than they were in 1991 by about 50% in real dollars. We are living the consequences of this reality today. Cutting back on everything from free peanuts to checked bags and outsourcing functions like maintenance and customer service to the lowest bidder, the industry is fundamentally different than 20 years ago.

---

[2] "Oh What a Lovely Fare War," *BusinessWeek*, June 29, 1992.

[3] Ibid.

A key part of this shift is the transformation of the public's perception of air travel. Before '92, the vast majority of travelers viewed the major carriers and the experience as something akin to a luxury item. In marketing, which at its core is the direction a company takes to deliver its products and services to the marketplace, luxury items are the most desirous to sell. Loyalty can be more easily built and maintained with customers who are willing to absorb higher prices. At this level, customers look forward to the introduction of new services and products. Price is not the determining factor. Relationships are the centerpiece and get cultivated over the long term. Building a cadre of premium customers ensures a sustainable business model. Retailers like Tiffany's are noteworthy for selling products that cater to the wants of high-end customers. If it's wrapped in the signature blue box with a white ribbon and sold only by Tiffany's at their stores or through their web site, it's an exclusive product that can command an optimum price.

After the deep discounts of 1992, the ability to sell premium customers on the added-value of the airline experience got much, much harder for the major carriers. Again from the practice of marketing we learn that at the moment a premium customer sees the product they are loyal to become deep-discounted, the esteem that was held for that product is lost. The unique brand becomes merely a commodity. Unfortunately, this is an all-too-common occurrence in business today. It is not unique to the airline industry. Selling through low-cost mega-retailers like Wal-Mart has turned long-standing brands like Levi's, Rubbermaid, and Goodyear into shells of their former selves. And you can't put the toothpaste back in the tube, as the cliché goes, if you later decide you made a mistake.

Imagine if Tiffany's set up a counter at Wal-Mart. How long would it take before the Tiffany's brand, even with the blue box and white ribbon, became merely a commodity in the eyes of its best customers? Even the venerable Apple is playing a dangerous game right now by expanding its sales through Wal-Mart, Best Buy, and other huge chains. One wonders if they will be able to keep the barbarians at the gate and hold onto their image as a hip, cutting-edge, innovative company. Or, will they too fall victim to the trap of big volume and discounts? The fact is that once the perception of the product is diminished in the eyes of the customer, price becomes the primary factor that determines whether they buy it or not.

For the airlines, as time went on, any customer loyalty that remained was increasingly based on the traveler's proximity to a hub, not really anything else. For example, I live in Cleveland. As it emerged from bankruptcy, Continental became the major carrier here, operating one of its three hubs at Hopkins International: the others being in Newark and Houston. The economy in

Northeastern Ohio has been tough for more than 30 years. The population has barely grown. Many good jobs have left. Still, despite the constant economic challenges, the state and local governments, along with occasional support from the feds, have done all they can—and probably more—to incentivize the airline to keep its operations here. The airport, which is owned by the City of Cleveland, has been remodeled several times in recent years; runways have been expanded; and a new terminal, just for Continental flights, was added a little more than a decade ago. In addition, big tax breaks and subsidies have been handed out to the carrier from the State of Ohio, Cuyahoga County, and the City of Cleveland. Having Continental here is a big plus—and the politicians know it. The presence of the hub keeps us a "major league city"—despite the terrible history of our sports franchises. It also gives the nearly 4 million residents in the region great access to the global airline network. The airline's pay-off came in the form of customers like me who faithfully flew the carrier, bought a President's Club Membership, used the Continental MasterCard, and fought hard to get enough miles each year to make it to Gold Status. I would pay a bit more and even take a little longer trip if necessary so long as I could stay on Continental.

Recently, however, United has taken over Continental, and the future of the Cleveland hub is in grave danger. Already, many flights have been eliminated, ticket prices have risen, and it just seems a matter of time before I will have to connect through O'Hare in Chicago or Dulles in Washington, D.C.— United's hubs—to get anywhere. As a result, I, along with a lot of people like me, have begun to expand my comfort zone with other carriers. I now increasingly use Air Tran out of the Canton-Akron Airport when the price and connection is better, although it is a farther drive from my home. Although I still have the Continental MasterCard and my President's Club membership, I have resigned myself to not making Gold this year. Who knows what I will do next year when it comes time to renew?

This illustrates the fickle nature of most airline customers in the era of Flying Cheap. As the experience is pretty much the same across the industry; in other words, flying is now a commodity. The only real differentiators now for passengers are how low can the fare go, and does it fit into my schedule at this particular moment in time? As people worth their salt in marketing will tell you, it's very, very difficult to build a sustainable business with customers who are overwhelmingly price-sensitive and transaction-focused.

What about First Class and Business Class Passengers?

Within the total population of air travelers, first-class and business-class passengers are outliers. They are much smaller in number than the average airline passenger, and because of the extremely high fares they pay, absolutely critical to the overall well being of the industry. The conventional wisdom holds that if a typical flight is able to maximize revenues at the front of the plane, it will turn a profit. True, but it's a lot easier said than done.

During the economic boom of the mid-to-late 1990s, business and first-class passengers helped keep the airlines alive. It was not uncommon for a premium passenger to willingly pay 10-15 times more for his ticket than an economy class counterpart. However, when the stock market tanked in early 2000, business travel dried up, and so did the airline's last resort. As the economy rebounded in the middle part of the new decade, business-class travel picked up, but only slightly. It fell off the cliff when the financial crisis went into full swing in 2009. Although premium travelers have crept back since then, it has become apparent to the industry that building dependencies around the uncertainty of premium customers isn't a viable strategy for the future.

Where Is the Soft Landing?

Given the price-driven nature of economy class passengers and the unpredictability that surrounds the higher-end first and business class fliers, you might wonder how can I honestly say the industry is currently experiencing a soft landing; that, despite all of the threats from geopolitical events, terrorists, fluctuating fuel prices, economic uncertainty, and political action—or inaction—the industry is positioned for relatively consistent and predictable stability in the coming years. When it comes to passengers, the industry's current soft landing stems from the closing of The Expectation Gap and the unbundling of different products and services. These factors, along with The Outsourcing Compulsion, which makes up the second piece of the Flying Cheap strategy and is detailed in the next chapter, are forming the foundation for a stable airline industry that will service an increasingly larger number of human beings every year. Notice I didn't mention *profitable*. I said *stable*. A woeful lack of long-term profits is a constant for the industry and always will be. Only fools try to change history. Successful people learn from it.

The Expectation Gap and Air Travel

Twenty years have passed since the Summer of '92, and tens of millions of passengers only know that air travel is a lot like riding the bus. These new travelers are simply unaware of the past era of relative luxury and status. Moreover, for those of us old enough to remember what it was like in the pre-commoditization period, we have had ample time to adjust our expectations to the new paradigm. These are seminal shifts in the business of air travel. People are increasingly not looking to be coddled, handled with kid gloves, and made to feel like their air experience must be memorable. Rather, as Ryanair CEO Michael O'Leary suggests, today's passengers are hardy beasts—parsimonious when buying a ticket, profligate once in the air—willing to endure discomfort and indignity just so long as they get to their destination cheaply and with their suitcases.[4]

Among the most powerful forces in our lives are expectations. Some expectations come from other people: spouses, peers, bosses, friends, parents, children, suppliers, neighbors, customers, and plenty of others who all have their expectations of us. They expect certain things regarding our speech, our behavior, and our character. Additional expectations come more clearly from within us. We accept certain norms, and we expect ourselves to follow them. We prize certain goals and expect to realize them. One of the biggest sources of problems in business can come from what I call The Expectation Gap. Simply put, it is the difference between that which is imagined and the reality that emerges.

How many of us know someone who, when they got married, had unrealistic expectations of their new spouse? Even though the new spouse had a history of financial problems, drug abuse, or other big issues, the other party expected that marriage would change them. But, after a few years, little was different. And this is where The Expectation Gap sets in. Divorce became inevitable, something that could have been both predicted and avoided years before.

In business, it can be especially acute. We expect "just-in-time" to be exactly that. We expect our co-workers and subordinates to do things as we would. We expect the boss will appreciate our extra efforts and dedication. We expect the new IT system will finally make everything work seamlessly. When these things don't happen, we get the outcomes from the Gap: anger,

---

[4] Felix Gillette, "Ryanair's O'Leary Mulls One-Euro Toilets, Standing Passengers," Bloomberg, September 2, 2010, www.bloomberg.com/news/2010-09-02/ryanair-s-o-leary-ponders-pay-toilets-standing-passengers-in-profit-quest.html

lost customers, low employee morale, a growing credibility shortage, shrinking productivity, etc. Critical to managing The Expectation Gap is realism. This doesn't mean we should lower the bar and not expect ourselves and others to perform at high levels. Rather, we should maturely recognize the flaws inherent in any human endeavor—including air travel—and plan accordingly, especially in an increasingly complex world.

To their credit, passengers, sometime with the help of the airlines, have overwhelmingly begun to accept the reality of what it all means: that modern air travel is cruising the skies in a bus, and the best we should hope for is a cheap, safe, and uneventful experience. Southwest Airlines is famous for poking fun at the rigors and stress of air travel with its sarcastic safety lectures and in-cabin antics, as well as its advertising. Every customer contact point with the airline is meant to manage The Expectation Gap, so that there are very few surprises or major disappointments when something goes wrong. The passengers, the airline, and its employees are pretty much on the same page when it comes to their expectations.

Delta recently raised awareness of realistic expectations by creating an animated series of entertaining videos showing passengers confronted with delicate social situations. "Planeguage: The language of traveling by plane" is a series of 25 humorous videos the airline has posted online. The snippets include "Middleman," about the middle-seat bully; "Kidtastrophe," depicting unruly tots on planes; "Lav Dance," about the person who bumps into everyone in the airplane aisle while returning from the lavatory; and "Shady Lady," about the passenger who raises or closes the window shade without considering other passengers. Such marketing techniques are exponentially different than the luxurious-type experience that was pushed on the public just a few years ago. They show progress in the development and maturity of the airline industry. Knowing who you truly are as a business is the first step on the path to stability. It seems the industry may have finally figured it out.

Unbundling of Different Products and Services

In 2010, the U.S. airlines collected $3.4 billion in checked-bag fees. The 24% increase from 2009 revealed how the airlines are increasingly reliant on charging for once-free services to make money—and managing the risks posed by outside factors. Checked-bag fees—typically $50 round-trip for the first piece of checked luggage—are becoming the norm for the industry. "If it weren't for the fees, the airlines would most likely be losing money," said Jim Corridore, an airline analyst with Standard & Poor's.[5] Delta generated the most revenue from bag fees—$952 million—followed by the combined United and Continental at nearly $655 million. American collected $580 million and US Airways $513 million.[6] Under the philosophy of Flying Cheap, as oil prices rose quickly in 2009 and 2010 and fare increases couldn't keep up with the price of jet fuel, fees became a staple of the carriers. "Unfortunately for the airlines, when they try to roll $50 into the ticket prices, people stop buying tickets," said Rick Seaney, CEO of FareCompare.com.[7]

Buoyed by the success with checked-bag fees, the airlines are now charging for all sorts of extras, and passengers seem more than willing to accept it, so long as the price of a ticket stays low. As Tom Parsons, CEO of discount airfares site BestFares.com, observed, "We are truly going to an á la carte system. It's down to the nickel and dime from here on out."[8] The following sections cover some sources of new revenue that the airlines have already jumped into or are seriously considering for the near future.

Buying Your Ticket with a Credit Card

Most of the airlines have gone to cashless cabins, requiring a credit card for all purchases. But that pro-credit movement in the skies doesn't mean they can't ding you for booking a ticket with a credit card. This would entail charging something like a processing fee to cover the costs of using the card, plus a little more to make it worthwhile. One possible break could come for people with airline-branded credit cards. Delta and Continental already waive most baggage fees for passengers with their cards. There might be a similar waiver of this fee. Otherwise, the only way to avoid it is buying your tickets in cash at the airport or possibly using a third-party site like PayPal. But carrying cash around is a bit risky and paying in cash might label you a terrorist. It never seems to end...

---

[5] Scott Mayerowitz, "US Airlines Collected $3.4 Billion in Bag Fees in 2010," *Associated Press*, accessed June 13, 2011 at www.miamiherald.com/2011/06/14/v-print/2265221/us-airlines-collected-34b-in-bag.html#ixzz1Q2mzm6wc.

[6] Ibid.

[7] Ibid.

[8] Ibid.

Booking Fee

Except for Southwest Airlines, every major airline charges a fee to book a flight over the phone. The worst offenders are Delta Air Lines, Frontier, and United Airlines, which charge $25 or more per ticket. Third-party travel sites like Expedia and Orbitz charge around $7 per ticket for online booking.

Moreover, Ryanair charges 5 Euros per passenger each way to "cover costs associated" with its booking system. Several years ago, US Airways briefly charged $5 for booking online; Allegiant Airlines also charges an online booking fee ($14.99).

Choosing a Seat Fee

Opt to stretch out in an exit row and it'll cost you. AirTran charges a flat $20 each way for those seats, while United charges anywhere from $14 to $109 per flight. Even if you aren't angling for extra legroom, you can get charged just for choosing a seat. Spirit Airlines assesses a $15 fee to passengers who choose a window seat, $12 for an aisle, and $5 for one in the middle.

Check-in Fee

Airlines want passengers to use those airport kiosks or online check-in for everything. And there's a good reason for it: they save money by having to hire fewer people to work the counters or the phones. Ryanair already charges a 40 Euro fee—the airline calls it a "penalty"—for those passengers who need to have their boarding pass reissued at the airport. Spirit is considering a new fee to talk with a human at the airport.

Boarding Pass Fee

Spirit recently announced it will charge a $5 fee for passengers who ask an agent to print their boarding pass at the airport. You can bypass the fee by checking in online and printing your own boarding pass, or by checking in at an airport kiosk—for now. (Starting in 2012 boarding passes at airport kiosks will cost $1.) The new policy applies to all domestic and international flights booked on or after Tuesday for travel on November 1, 2011 and beyond. At the same time, Spirit says it is lowering fares on all nonstop flights by $5 each way. It's the first U.S. carrier to charge a boarding pass fee. In Europe, Ryanair has a similar, though more expensive, policy.

According to the airline, Spirit is just listening to its customers. In a customer survey, most told the carrier that they preferred lower fares in exchange for checking in online. "We want to give [passengers] the ability to choose the extras they want without forcing them to pay for add-ons they don't want or need," Ben Baldanza, the president and CEO of Spirit, said in a statement. "By lowering the fare for everyone and then charging only those who choose us to print their boarding pass, we let the customer decide. It's all about consumer choice."

Redeeming Frequent-Flier Miles Fee

"Some people have been collecting miles for years, and now they have to pay extra to use them," Parsons said.[9] US Airways charges $25 to $50 for you to book a flight using frequent-flier miles. American Airlines charges $5. On October 1, the airline began charging new fees for rewards upgrades ($50 to upgrade from coach to first class on a domestic flight, for instance) and higher mile requirements (a round-trip ticket to Europe costs 20,000 more miles). Worse, it's extremely tough for frequent fliers to redeem their miles now that airlines have cut back on flights, Parsons says.

Carry-on Luggage Fee

Spirit is accustomed to being in the news for its fees and advertising campaigns. Last year, the airline became the first carrier in the United States to implement a fee for carry-ons. In March, it added fees for travelers who wait to pay for carry-on or checked luggage within 24 hours of departure. The airline says it made this policy in order to speed up the boarding process.

Changing a Ticket Fee

Presently, Southwest is the only airline that doesn't charge domestic ticket holders for altering an itinerary. Change a flight on any other airline and you can expect to pay a fee ranging from $75 (Alaska Airlines, for online changes) to $150 (American, Continental, United, and US Airways).

Curbside Baggage Check

Don't feel like rolling your suitcases inside the terminal? Get your wallet out. Currently, Northwest and US Airways charge $2 per bag for curbside check-in. Others will be sure to follow.

---

[9] Ibid.

In-Flight Amenities

Forget about relaxing with a complementary blanket, soft pillow, and a cold drink. US Airways, for example, now charges $2 for nonalcoholic drinks. Be prepared to get hit in other ways. Want a pillow and blanket on your Jet-Blue flight? That'll be $7.

Checked Bag Fees by the Pound

Right now most airlines charge a fee for checked bags and then additional fees for overweight bags. For instance, Delta charges $25 for the first checked bag ($23 if you pre-purchase on the Internet) for luggage up to 50 pounds. Passengers with bags weighing 51 to 70 pounds get hit with an additional $90 fee. Those with bags weighing 71 to 100 pounds face $175.

No More Price-Drop Refunds

It's a little-known trick in the airline world, but passengers can often rebook their exact same flights if the price drops after they make a purchase. Alaska, JetBlue, and Southwest don't charge anything to take advantage of a price drop, while other airlines charge $75 to $150 for domestic tickets and more for international flights. So the price needs to drop more than the change fee in order for you to reap any advantage from the lower fare. None of the airlines actually gives you cash back; instead you get a credit good for travel on one of their flights in the next 12 months.

Infant Fees

Right now, children under the age of two who sit on their parents' laps fly for free. The National Transportation Safety Board wants to change that. The federal agency says that a large number of airplane crashes are actually survivable, but only if everybody is buckled up. And as much as a mother or father might love their child, it is highly unlikely that they will be able to hold on tight enough during a crash to stop the baby from flying through the cabin. Ryanair already charges 20 Euros for lap children.

A Pay as You "Go" Fee?

This is actually an idea that has been floating around for a few years, ever since Ryanair said it would consider charging for the bathrooms. It hasn't yet happened in Europe and probably won't be coming to the U.S. anytime soon. Nevertheless, given the current trajectory, we may yet see it in our lifetime...

Leveraging Technology and Regaining Control

Over the past decade, the airlines have been empowered to better manage this new customer relationship management approach through the successful deployment of information technology. It is here where advances in data collection and analysis aligned with a realistic vision of the future provide the industry with the new way forward that is known as Flying Cheap. But before this could occur, the airlines needed wrestle control of their sales and distribution away from the all-powerful network of travel agents.

Until recently, the majority of airline passengers purchased their tickets through a global network of travel agents. Working on behalf of the airlines, travel agents controlled the flow of information between the two parties. As is often the case, the middlemen became more and more powerful as time went on. Think about the auto industry. Who is really in charge? Is it the manufacturers who invest all of the blood, sweat, tears, and money to create new innovations and models each year? Or, is it really the dealers, many of which represent multiple manufacturers and brands? The biggest car dealer in America is AutoNation. They sell cars like Wal-Mart sells dish soap: multiple brands on the same platform treated the same and differentiated primarily by price. The airlines, always needing to fill seats, would regularly incentivize the travel agents to push sales onto passengers. Of course, the travel agents sold tickets for almost every airline. So, the travel agents were able to play one off against another to get the best deals for themselves.

This ability of the travel agencies to effectively control the number of passengers on a given flight gave them tremendous power and made it much harder for the airlines to manage their cost structures. This dysfunctional relationship continued for decades until the advent of the Internet. It was at this moment that the airlines saw a way out of the trap they were in—and they jumped at it. Between 1999 and 2009, the airlines steadily chopped away at the commissions they paid to the travel agents and sought to push passengers to use new electronic channels to buy their tickets. In this period, upward of 75,000 travel agents were thrown out of work, and thousands of agencies were shuttered.[10] By 2006, most of the major carriers had

---

[10] U.S. Department of Labor, Bureau of Labor Statistics (all employees at U.S. travel agencies in August of each year).

cut travel agent commissions on domestic flights completely. And by 2009, more than half of all airline reservations were made online.[11] Increasingly, those online reservations are being made on the home page of the airlines themselves. Through the establishment of a direct relationship with a growing number of their passengers, the airlines have been able to gain critical data that has enabled them to be much more efficient in the operations.

Improving Passenger Load Factors

If you've noticed that your recent flights have been packed and lacking empty seats, you've spotted a rising trend in the industry—and a big part of the Flying Cheap strategy. As the airlines have gleaned more information about their passengers and turned a lot of it into knowledge, the industry has been able to dramatically increase its passenger load factor (PLF). PLF is a measurement that the airlines use to determine the amount of utilization of the total available capacity of a flight. Simply stated, a higher PLF means there are a lot of "butts in the seats." A low PLF means a lot passengers are traveling disguised as empty seats. Clearly, the airlines want high PLFs.

By better knowing who their passengers are and studying behavior patterns, the airlines have been able to learn which flights are strong and which ones need help to get the PLF up. This knowledge ultimately provides the airlines with the ability to better manage its fuel and labor costs, the largest expenses the industry has. The industry has done this very well, as 2010-11 was the period with the highest PLF in history. According to the U.S. Department of Transportation, the average passenger load factor for all U.S. carriers in July 2011 was a whopping 89.6%.[12]

Many industry analysts argue that PLF is probably one of the most important indicators of the overall health of the industry. Given the industry's unquestionable success in ramping up its PLF, we can conclude that things look much better than a few years, where PLFs averaged around 50-60%.

So What Does This Mean for Passengers?

While increased PLFs have been a huge win for the industry and supports the soft landing, it has made the air travel experience more difficult for passengers. As the airlines now have the upper hand, passengers are at the

---

[11] Forester Research, "U.S. Online Travel Forecast," January 20, 2009.

[12] U.S. Department of Transportation, Bureau of Transportation Statistics, July 2011 PLFs.

behest of quick decisions by the airlines. The ability to learn from the data allows airlines to almost instantaneously re-price a flight, overbook it, or even cancel it. And while this is in the interest of the airline, being stranded after a cancellation or not being allowed to board despite having a ticket and seat assignment is a greater possibility for passengers.

At its core, the passenger side of the Flying Cheap strategy represents the ability of the airline industry to better manage the expectations of its customers, charge higher and higher fees for previously uncharged services, and better handle the capacity of their flights. It provides a type of insurance against the external factors that regularly impact the industry. To date, governments around the world have not intervened in this part of the Flying Cheap strategy. They have sat on the sidelines. Some passenger rights groups have questioned where all this is headed, but no real legislation or new regulation appears on the horizon. It appears that this model is here to stay for the foreseeable future.

Flying Cheap, Part 2

The Outsourcing Compulsion

"In theory, there is no difference between practice and theory. In practice, there is a difference."

—Attributed to Yogi Berra

If you live long enough, you'll notice that what is the latest and greatest today is merely a current version of something you've experienced in the past. In the late 1980s, America was in a funk. Fears were rampant that the country was losing its competitive advantage. The economy was stagnant. Jobs were being shipped overseas in huge numbers. It seemed the American Dream was falling by the wayside as Japan—yes, Japan—was destined to become the nation that would now dominate the world.

Fearing the demise of the Republic is nothing new in America. Americans are prone to an almost inexplicable belief in our inevitable decline. Right after winning our War of Independence, many of the Founding Fathers worried about America going the way of the Roman Empire. As the incomparable English writer Charles Dickens observed in the middle of the 19th century, "If its individual citizens, to a man, are to be believed, America always is depressed, and always is stagnated, and always is in an alarming crisis, and never was otherwise." On the positive side of things, this apparently natural pessimism about the current state of things always keeps America and Americans on the edge, ever ready to explore new ideas and options.

In the face of supposedly unstoppable Japanese ascendancy 25 years ago, well-meaning business gurus offered a long list of possible solutions for how American companies could turn things around. Organizational transformation emphasizing things like resources, capabilities, innovation, technology, and operational effectiveness was preached from the highest heights as the way to beat back the Japanese threat. Of all of the potential answers, the most influential came in a 1990 *Harvard Business Review* article by C.K. Prahaldad and Gary Hamel entitled "The Core Competence of the Corporation." The idea was pretty simple: the successful company of the future will be built around a core of shared competencies (in other words, those parts of the business that bring value to customers and the corporation). Taken to its logical conclusion, the Core Competence Theory, as it came to be known, compelled business leaders to identify the activities and functions that *don't* bring value and outsource them. For example, why have an in-house payroll department or customer service call center if, instead, you can outsource those tasks, so you can dedicate more attention to the things that really make money like innovative new products and services?

Over the past 20 years, the Core Competence Theory has become a mainstay of business education; and, not surprisingly, outsourcing has surged. Wrapped in the blanket of building better "efficiencies" and, therefore, ultimately lowering costs to consumers, outsourcing has been touted by free market proponents as *the* way forward for organizational success. Of course, efficiency itself is not a bad objective to strive for. We have all benefitted from improvements in efficiencies in areas like personal computing and mobile telephony. The problem arises when the unrestrained drive for efficiencies combines with outsourcing to produce a race to the bottom.

If you sense here that I am not a big fan of the practice of outsourcing, you'd be right. A recent book of mine tore apart the application of Core Competency Theory in the real world.[1] Outsourcing some functions does make sense. However, companies frequently went too far and outsourced things they should never have. For example, the rise of mega-distributors like Wal-Mart has shifted the power away from companies who innovate and produce products to the retailers who sell them. Wal-Mart has about 125,000 suppliers. Because of its size, the retailer is the largest customer for the vast majority of those producers. In the lexicon of efficiency, it makes sense to

---

[1] Andrew R. Thomas and Timothy J. Wilkinson, *The Distribution Trap: Keeping Your Innovations from Becoming Commodities* (Santa Barbara, CA: ABC-CLIO, 2010).

deal with one customer like Wal-Mart. Yet, ask most of those suppliers how their profits stack up with Wal-Mart's year after year and you'll likely hear anything but nice words.

Wal-Mart's inevitable price cuts force inefficiencies to be squeezed out of the system, which does lower the cost to consumers. But the constant hammering to lower the price often forces suppliers to leave the U.S. and chase cheaper labor costs around the world. Because they can't sell their products for more money, the only option is to reduce operating expenses. The cost of the benefit in lower prices at places like Wal-Mart is good-paying American jobs. The lesson is that once you get on the outsourcing treadmill, it is very difficult get off. It is very hard to make a lasting compromise between efficiency and anything else, because the quest for greater efficiency—and lower costs—is by far the more powerful force.

Outsourcing and the Airline Industry

It almost goes without saying that the people who run the major airlines viscerally understand that the industry has not ever really been profitable and probably never will be. Nevertheless, as corporate officers, they also know there is a fiduciary responsibility on their part to act in the best interests of the company's shareholders. This legal mandate compels them to look at ways in which they can provide returns to their investors. As any first-year business undergraduate can tell you, there are only two ways for a company to make money: increase profits or cut costs. Further, although the low-cost carriers gained market share and customer loyalty during the last 20 years, they are also fighting against surging fuel prices, security threats, and all the unpredictability and realities of the industry's operating environment.

Not surprisingly, as the Core Competence Theory gained traction, leaders across the airline industry took a long, hard look at the outsourcing option. Almost right away, the result was a rapid reduction of functions performed by the airlines and their own employees. Look out the window on your next flight while the plane is sitting at the gate and you can observe outsourcing in action: the catering service vehicles and fuel trucks are not owned or operated by the airlines. Providing food and fueling up jets are contracted out to third parties who do the work in exchange for a fee paid by the airlines. No big thing; it makes sense. But what about your pilot and co-pilot: are they employees of the airline or are they working for a low-cost contracting outfit? How about the maintenance of the plane you're flying on? Who's doing the work: the airline or a low-cost offshore facility?

The Outsourcing of Whole Airlines

"On February 12, 2009, about 2217 eastern standard time, a Colgan Air, Inc., Bombardier DHC-8-400, N200WQ, operating as Continental Connection flight 3407, was on an instrument approach to Buffalo-Niagara International Airport, Buffalo, New York, when it crashed into a residence in Clarence Center, New York, about 5 nautical miles northeast of the airport. The 2 pilots, 2 flight attendants, and 45 passengers aboard the airplane were killed, 1 person on the ground was killed, and the airplane was destroyed by impact forces and a post-crash fire."[2] These are the words of the National Transportation Safety Board's (NTSB) investigation report.

Let's look closer at the phrase "*operating as Continental Connection flight 3407.*" What does this mean? It seems that the pilots were not Continental employees. And the plane they were flying, although painted in Continental colors, was not owned and operated by Continental. Instead, the pilots were employees of and the aircraft was owned by Colgan Air, a contractor that flies routes for US Airways, United, and Continental.[3] Colgan Air is a regional carrier.

If you fly commercially in the United States, there is about a 1 in 2 chance that you will be traveling on a regional carrier. Every day in America there are approximately 13,000 flights on regional carriers, representing roughly half of all commercial flight activity.[4] In Europe, about 16 percent of all daily flights are on regional carriers.[5] Regional carriers are just that: regional. They provide the feeder flights from lower-populated regions and airports to the hubs of the major carriers. In the cost-driven mindset that is the modern day airline industry, regional carriers serve a huge purpose. Former Continental CEO Gordon Bethune was a leader in leveraging outsourcing. Outsourcing to regional carriers helped Continental remain more competitive and avoid

---

[2] U.S. National Transportation Safety Report, NTSB Document ID #DCA09MA027, Washington, DC, 2009.

[3] The Public Broadcasting Service (PBS) did a *Frontline* special entitled "Flying Cheap," which broadcast in January 2011. The focus was on the outsourcing aspect of the airline industry's strategy today. The URL for the online version is www.pbs.org/wgbh/pages/frontline/flyingcheap/etc/synopsis.html.

The notion of "Flying Cheap" has been around for quite a while. The originator of the term is unknown. I publically first used it and the comparison with modern day air travel to Wal-Mart in a February 22, 2008, MSNBC article written by Karen Aho and entitled "The Death of the Airline Meal." The URL for that article is http://articles.moneycentral.msn.com/SavingandDebt/TravelForLess/TheDeathOfTheAirlineMeal.aspx.

[4] Regional Airline Association, Industry Statistics, www.raa.org.

[5] European Regions Airline Association, Industry Statistics, www.eraa.org/index.php.

another bankruptcy as they bid more routes out. "Having an independent allows an airline to bid that and have a competitive relationship and make sure they get their flying done at the lowest cost," explains Bethune.[6] Like Continental, the others majors are able to outsource this "non-value" portion of their business to the more efficient regionals, allowing the major to focus on their "core competencies"—flying bigger planes and longer flights out of their hubs.

Within the industry-speak of the airlines, the term "code-share" is what defines the relationship between the majors and the outsourced regionals. These agreements between the two parties allow the major carrier to streamline the experience for the consumer and better manage costs. One of the key aspects of code-share contracts is to assure carrier continuity. They include very specific provisions that make it virtually impossible for the public to differentiate between the regional contracting airline, like Colgan, and the major carrier, like Continental. Everything from the logo and colors of the airplanes to the staff uniforms to the free magazines stashed in the seat in front of you carry the branding of the major. Table 5-1 shows the major carriers and the contractors.

Table 5-1. U.S. Major Carriers, Their Outsourced Brands, and Contractors. (Source: OAG Schedules, February 2011)

Major Carrier	Outsourced Brand	Contractor
Alaska Airlines	N/A	Horizon Air Peninsula
Air Tran Airways	N/A	SkyWest Airlines
American Airlines	American Eagle	American Eagle American Eagle / Executive
	American Connection	Chautauqua Airlines
Continental Airlines	Continental Express	Chautauqua Airlines Express Jet
	Continental Connection	Cape Air Colgan Air CommutAir Gulfstream International

---

[6] "Flying Cheap," PBS *Frontline,* January 2011.

Major Carrier	Outsourced Brand	Contractor
Delta Airlines	N/A	Atlantic Southwest Chautauqua Airlines Comair Compass Airlines Mesaba Airlines Pinnacle Airlines Shuttle America SkyWest Airlines
Jet Blue Airways	N/A	Cape Air
United Airlines	United Express	Atlantic Southeast Colgan Air ExpressJet Airlines GoJet Airlines Great Lakes Mesa Airlines Shuttle America SkyWest Airlines Trans States Airlines
US Airways	US Airways Express	Air Wisconsin Chautauqua Airlines Colgan Air Mesa Airlines Piedmont PSA Republic Airlines Trans States Airlines

Like much of outsourcing across the business spectrum, the efficiency of the regionals is primarily found in lower cost structures, especially for human labor. Rebecca Shaw, the 24-year old co-pilot of the "Continental" flight that crashed outside of Buffalo, earned $16,524 a year from Colgan Air. A resident of Seattle, Ms. Shaw earned less working for the Virginia-based contractor as a pilot than had she stayed home, continued living with her parents, and worked 40 hours a week for minimum wage, which is $8.67 an hour in Washington. Even more disturbing, the night prior to the crash, Ms. Shaw commuted as a passenger on an overnight flight from Seattle to Memphis and then caught a connection to reach her base airport in Newark, where Flight 3047 originated. The NTSB reported that Ms. Shaw had sent text messages throughout the day that she did not feel well. The NTSB said Shaw had once held a second job in a coffee shop while working as a pilot for Colgan in Norfolk, Virginia. NTSB investigators said 93 of the 137 Colgan pilots who worked out of Newark at the time of the accident were commuting from far away, including 29 living more than 1,000 miles away.[7] Bill Voss, president of the Flight Safety Foundation, raises some valid concerns about outsourcing to the regionals when he states: "There are some accidents that really make you step back and take a look at what's happening in the system. [Flight] 3407 forces us to look at issues like commuting, fatigue. It forces us to look at training. It forces us to look at fundamental regulatory relationships. It's a very important event."[8]

The Outsourcing of Aircraft Maintenance

When reading the outsourcing menu, the huge savings associated with maintenance costs clearly stands out. If an airline fixes its own planes using its own employees in the U.S., it spends about $100 per hour for every union mechanic, including wages, benefits, and other costs. If, instead, the airline chooses to use an outsourced, non-unionized contractor in the U.S. to do the same work, the airline will save about 50 percent. If the carrier decides to use a firm outside the United States, the cost savings can be as high as 75 percent. Predictably, in the era of Flying Cheap, the airline industry is now sending most of its planes to be overhauled and fixed at private repair shops both in the U.S. and overseas. When passengers board a commercial flight today, there is an over 50 percent probability that the maintenance on their U.S. aircraft was performed not by FAA-certificated mechanics employed by an airline, but instead by workers at one of nearly 5,000 domestic and foreign contract repair stations.

According to the Department of Transportation Office of Inspection General, major air carriers outsourced an average of 64 percent of their maintenance expenses in 2007, compared to only 37 percent in 1996.[9] This work includes everything from repairing critical components, such as landing gear and engine overhauls, to performing heavy airframe checks. Further, in the 2008 report, the nine air carriers that were reviewed sent 71 percent of their heavy airframe maintenance checks to contract maintenance providers in calendar year 2007, up from 34 percent in 2003.[10] In

---

[7] U.S. National Transportation Safety Report, NTSB Document ID #DCA09MA027, 2009, Washington, DC.

[8] Ibid.

[9] "Air Carriers' Outsourcing of Aircraft Maintenance," Federal Aviation Administration Report Number: AV-2008-090, Date Issued: September 30, 2008, Washington, DC.

[10] Ibid.

what is becoming increasingly the norm with outsourcing in all industries, overseas firms are becoming viable alternatives. In fact, foreign repair stations completed 246 (27 percent) of these carriers' 907 heavy airframe maintenance checks outsourced in 2007, up from 21 percent in 2003. There are roughly 700 FAA-approved repair companies in other countries—including repair shops in Argentina, Costa Rica, Ethiopia, Kenya, China, and Indonesia.[11]

Can We Trust the FAA to Properly Regulate and Oversee All This Outsourcing?

When an airline uses a contractor that is certified by the FAA to fly under its banner or maintain or fix its equipment, the contractor becomes an extension of the airline itself. At least in theory, the activity is to be treated the same by the governmental regulator, regardless of who is performing the service or where it is being done. But in practice, things don't work quite as well. They never do. The FAA says it has about 4,300 inspectors responsible for aviation safety, overseeing flight operations, pilot certifications, maintenance, and manufacturers. But ever since deregulation, federal auditors, including the U.S. Government Accountability Office and the Department of Transportation's Office of the Inspector General, have routinely raised questions about the FAA's ability to effectively watch over such a vast and dynamic industry.[12]

Regulating the Regionals

Six fatal regional airline accidents occurred between 2003 and 2009 in the U.S.—the Continental Flight 3407 Buffalo crash in February 2009 being the latest one—and questions are again being raised about the FAA. To better understand how the agency's resources are targeted, PBS's *Frontline* asked the FAA how many inspectors are assigned to oversee each commercial airline and how many of those are assigned to regional carriers. Surprisingly, the FAA says it doesn't have those numbers at headquarters and wouldn't be able to say how many inspectors are dedicated to overseeing the regional airline industry.[13]

---

[11] Ibid.

[12] Ibid.

[13] "Flying Cheap," PBS *Frontline*, January 2011.

It's particularly surprising because these questions aren't new. In 1992, after a similar string of regional accidents, there was a call for additional federal oversight over smaller airlines. The U.S. General Accounting Office released a report called "Commuter Airline Safety Would be Enhanced with Better FAA Oversight" that showed that accident rates had increased 67 percent between 1990 and 1991 and FAA inspectors weren't effectively uncovering safety violations. In response, the FAA beefed up its total inspector force, which now numbers about 70 percent more than in 1992. It also initiated a new inspection and enforcement approach called the Air Transportation Oversight System (ATOS) that was designed to improve its capabilities by more efficiently identifying and targeting the highest safety risks.[14]

But implementation of ATOS has been problematic. More than a decade after its initiation, the Inspector General of the Department of Transportation, Calvin L. Scovel III, says there are still serious deficiencies in the system. At a U.S. Senate hearing about FAA oversight following the Buffalo crash, Scovel testified that in 2005, inspectors failed to complete a quarter of their planned ATOS inspections—half of which were regarding previously identified risks. Moreover, Scovel said ATOS was designed to cover the major airlines and had not been widely adopted at the regional level. Not until recently did the majority of inspectors covering the regional airline industry begin using a risk-based system. Scovel said inspectors told his office that the system needed to be reconfigured to work with the regionals.[15]

In the case of Colgan Air, the National Transportation Safety Board recently raised concerns about the FAA's ability to effectively oversee the company during important periods of growth and expansion. In the year before the 3407 accident, Colgan added a fleet of new Bombardier Dash-8 Q400 turboprop planes, growing by 30 percent to satisfy a new contract with Continental. The addition required new pilots, new training for a much more sophisticated plane, and new safety manuals and procedures. However, the FAA added no inspectors to help survey Colgan's growth. Moreover, NTSB noted that the principal FAA inspector in charge was learning how to fly the new plane at the same time as the company's pilots.

---

[14] The three GAO reports referenced here include "Aviation Safety: Problems Persist with FAA's Inspection Program" (GAO/RCED-92-14, Nov. 20, 1991), "Aviation Safety: Emergency Revocation Orders of Air Carrier Certificates"(GAO/RCED-92-10, Oct. 17, 1991), and "Aviation Safety: Air Taxis--The Most Accident-Prone Airlines Need Better Oversight"(GAO/RED-92-60, Jan. 21, 1992).

[15] "Regional Air Carriers and Pilot Workforce Issues," Statement of The Honorable Calvin L. Scovel III Inspector General U.S. Department of Transportation, Committee on Transportation and Infrastructure Subcommittee on Aviation United States House of Representatives, June 11, 2009, CC-2009-075.

The NTSB concluded: "The current Federal Aviation Administration surveillance standards for oversight at air carriers undergoing rapid growth and increased complexity of operations do not guarantee that any challenges encountered by the carriers as a result of these changes will be appropriately mitigated."[16]

Regulating Outsourced Maintenance

When a U.S. airline sends planes to a repair shop, whether in the U.S. or another country, the work is supposed to be supervised by FAA-certified mechanics and then checked by inspectors with the repair company, the airline, and the FAA. To be sure, it is a difficult task, and one that requires constant vigilance. The Inspector General of the Department of Transportation investigated those checks and balances and warned that FAA and industry inspectors were not monitoring the work the way they should. Although written in the dry bureaucratic language of Washington, DC, the findings provide a window into how the FAA monitors the outsourcing of maintenance:[17]

> Our audit objectives were to (1) identify the type and quantity of maintenance performed by external repair stations and (2) determine whether FAA is effectively monitoring air carriers' oversight of external repair stations' work and verifying that safety requirements are met. We found that while FAA has begun moving its safety oversight toward a risk–based system, it still relies too heavily on air carriers' oversight procedures, which are not always sufficient.
>
> Specifically, we determined that FAA **did not** (1) have an adequate system for determining how much and where the most critical maintenance occurs, (2) have a specific policy governing when certificate management inspectors should visit repair stations performing substantial maintenance, (3) require inspectors to validate that repair stations have corrected deficiencies identified in air carrier audits, and (4) have adequate controls to ensure that inspectors document inspection findings in the national database and review related findings by other inspectors.

---

[16] U.S. National Transportation Safety Report, NTSB Document ID #DCA09MA027, 2009, Washington, DC.

[17] "Air Carriers' Outsourcing of Aircraft Maintenance," Federal Aviation Administration Report Number: AV-2008-090, Date Issued: September 30, 2008, Washington, DC.

As a result, FAA could not effectively target its inspection resources to those repair stations providing the highest volume of repairs, which caused deficiencies at repair stations to go undetected or reoccur and prevented inspectors from obtaining sufficient data to perform comprehensive risk assessments. We recommended that FAA develop and implement an effective system to determine how much and where critical maintenance is performed.

Even more disconcerting is that some foreign-based repair shops servicing U.S. airlines do not require the drug and alcohol screening mandated by the FAA for facilities in the United States.

"These findings are very, very disturbing," says John Goglia, a former presidential appointee to the National Transportation Safety Board. "If we're not monitoring them [outsourced maintenance facilities] properly, how do we know it's safe?" Goglia says the fact that there have been so few crashes in recent years masks a troubling trend that the public can't see as airlines have been slashing costs. "The margin of safety is getting thinner," he says. "The absence of an accident doesn't mean you're safe. We should be monitoring and doing our job before there's an accident, not after."[18]

In the end, all decisions have consequences, and the industry's embrace of outsourcing matters to everyone. On the security side of things, for example, despite legislative mandates to establish a security standard for repair stations and audit foreign stations, the Transportation Security Administration (TSA) has yet to do this. Because of these security—not safety— concerns, the FAA stopped processing all new applications for certification submitted by foreign repair stations after August 3, 2008.

With respect to personnel background checks, drug and alcohol testing, access to aircraft, and parts inventory, there is one standard for airline-owned maintenance facilities and domestic U.S. FAA-certificated repair stations, and no standard for foreign repair stations. There are few safeguards in place to prevent terrorists from exploiting an opportunity to do us harm by, for example, tampering with airline systems or inserting explosives into an aircraft while they are undergoing maintenance.

Further, outsourcing aircraft maintenance is decimating what will be a hard-to-replace national asset: highly skilled aircraft and avionics technicians. Once it is so cut down, this mission-critical workforce will be virtually impossible

---

[18] Daniel Zwerdling, "To Cut Costs, Airlines Send Repairs Abroad," *National Public Radio*, October 19, 2009, www.npr.org/templates/story/story.php?storyId=113877784.

to rebuild. The same has happened in American manufacturing. For example, as tool-and-die jobs became increasingly exported, the number of people in this country who can perform this vital service has become fewer and fewer.

Moreover, if we are going to depend upon the FAA and other federal agencies to provide the kind of flexible and comprehensive oversight of the industry we expect, changes are necessary. Unfortunately, as you'll see next, change is something easier said than done when it comes to governmental regulation of the airline industry. Further, if history is any indicator, this convoluted relationship could derail any soft landing.

The (D)evolution of Aviation Security and the Birth of the TSA

"The only thing you don't know is the history you haven't learned."

—Harry S. Truman

After World War II, as the pace of industry expansion accelerated and airliners became much more common in the sky, Congress felt it necessary to place all of the federal government's regulatory authority in the hands of a single agency. The Federal Aviation Act of 1958 transferred the regulatory functions of both the Civil Aeronautics Administration (CAA) and Civil Aeronautics Board (CAB) to a new, independent agency—the Federal Aviation Agency. In addition—and this is a big one—Congress gave the new agency another mandate: to advance the expansion of the civil aviation industry. The legislation was summarized as follows:

> *An act to continue the Civil Aeronautics Board as an agency of the United States to create a Federal Aviation Agency, to provide for the regulation and promotion [emphasis added] of civil aviation in such a manner as to best foster its development and safety.*[1]

In Title III of the bill, Section 305 elaborated. The FAA's responsibility to support air commerce was further defined:

> *The Administrator is empowered and directed to encourage and foster [emphasis added] the development of civil aeronautics and air commerce in the United States and abroad.*

Throughout its existence, the FAA would come to be defined as a federal agency that was torn apart by two competing and divergent goals. Asking a federal agency to regulate an industry it is also charged with promoting creates a basic conflict of interest and raises more questions than answers. Moreover, Congress never gave any parameters to the FAA to help the agency recognize where the line of promotion ended and where the line of regulation began. The agency was left to determine for itself the ways in which it worked with the industry. Ultimately, as a result of the conflicting Congressional imperatives, a regulatory body would emerge that would be first confused and later snarled by its own mission.

Market Forces Come to Dominate the FAA

As the aviation industry became more and more critical to the well-being of the U.S. economy, commercial interests began to take precedence over other concerns. Starting in the late 1960s, when FAA was moved from the Commerce Department to the newly created Department of Transportation and became the Federal Aviation Administration, the airlines, through intensive lobbying efforts on Capitol Hill, strove to ensure that their ultimate objectives were met. These objectives were more often in line with the "promotional" and commercial aspects of FAA's mission but were contrary to the safety and security mandates of the agency.

Aviation security, always the ugly step-child, was dragged along as a burden nobody really ever wanted to deal with—but had to. Until the terrorist attacks of September 11, 2001, civil aviation security was an often confused and contradictory combination of laws, regulations, and resources. The

---

[1] The complete reference for the Federal Aviation Act of 1958 is Public Law 85-726; 72 Stat. 737; 49 U.S.C. App. 1301 et. seq.

program was supposed to be a system of shared and complementary responsibilities involving the federal government, air carriers, passengers, and airports (Table 6-1). In theory, the FAA set the standards and guidelines, and air carriers and airports implemented them. And, if the guidelines and standards were not being followed by the carriers, the FAA was mandated to enforce the existing regimen. Passengers and the users of air cargo, who were the ultimate beneficiaries of the program, paid for aviation security through surcharges included in the price of airline tickets and cargo shipments.

Table 6-1. Theoretical Roles and Responsibilities of the Pre-9/11 Aviation Security System in the U.S.

FAA	AIRLINES	AIRPORTS
Make policy	Screen passengers	Protect air operations
Identify and assess threats	Screen baggage	Provide access control
Approve security plans	Screen cargo	Provide law enforcement
Inspect compliance	Guard aircraft	Dispose of explosives
Provide direction		
Initiate necessary changes		

And, although authority might be delegated or shared (i.e. a private security company might operate the security checkpoints), the ultimate responsibility for the safety and security of civil aviation was presumed to rest with the FAA.

As time went on, it became clear that Congress made a grievous error when it gave the agency the job of commercially promoting the same industry it was charged with regulating. It was, frankly, a bad idea. The "Dual Mandate," as it came to be called, was to define and shape the mission, goals, and actions of the FAA more than any other single factor throughout its existence. Moreover, it would eventually lead the agency, at the expense of the public welfare, into a position that allowed a culture of compromise to fester.

A Great Job Lobbying

To understand how market forces usurped the regulatory authority of the FAA when it came to aviation security on and before 9/11, we need only to look at who was working on behalf of the airlines and how much was spent to buy influence. Doing so reveals the scope of the airlines' reach into the FAA when it came to determining aviation security policy. It also reveals the extent to which the agency had become beholden to the industry it was supposed to be regulating.

Individuals or groups promoting special interests are as old as America itself. James Madison, in *Federalist #10*, recognized the reality that particular factions within society would always seek to advance their interests at the expense of others.

> *Liberty is to faction what air is to fire, a lament without which it instantly expires. But it could not be a less folly to abolish liberty, which is essential to political life, because it nourishes faction than it would be to wish the annihilation of air, which is essential to animal life, because it imparts to fire its destructive agency.*

Madison, like most of the Founding Fathers, believed that the limited and separated structure of the government they designed would naturally win out against those who wanted an activist government. However, Madison and many of his cohorts were wrong. What they failed to envision were the ways politicians, bureaucrats, and commercial interests dedicated to government action could manipulate the system to easily advance the desires of the few over those of the many. Naturally gridlocked, decentralized, divided, and weak government—the foundations of the Constitution—were in due time overcome by the energies of activism and centralization.

The efforts of the airline industry and the people who left government to influence policy decisions on its behalf are a striking example of what determined, well-connected, and well-financed lobbying can do. (You'll see a number of examples in a few pages.) In getting their way, the airlines showed they were much more successful at it than almost anybody else. When confronted with the tough decision of whether to side with public safety or align themselves with market forces, FAA most often chose to support the airlines, even when it flew in the face of logic and sound public policy.

It is important to recognize that market forces will always seek to dominate regulatory authority. Such a proposition is not exclusively endemic to commercial aviation. Whatever the enterprise, uncontrolled and unrestrained market forces will inevitably work toward commercial outcomes alone.

Whether it is in aviation, finance, chemicals, medicine, automobiles, or fabricating widgets, the drive for profits will always overshadow every other interest, including the public good. And, while the desire for profits allows talent, opportunity, and creativity to flourish, unregulated market forces in due time will swallow up everything else around them. This is the nature of unbridled capitalism at its core.

The linchpin in this difficult balancing act is the character of the individuals and organizations that operate within governmental agencies. Regulatory authority is only able to function effectively when civil servants, entrusted and paid by the people to guard the public interest, successfully ward off special interests and the formidable power of market forces. A breakdown at this level assures that commercial interests will penetrate and eventually jeopardize an agency's integrity. If market forces are permitted to move about unabated, the agency will eventually become compromised.

The revolving door of recent lobbyists for major U.S. airlines that have worked in the highest levels of government is truly a recent Who's Who list of Washington insiders. Just a few of the noteworthy names include:[2]

Table 6-2. Examples of the Revolving Door.

INDIVIDUAL	PAST EMPLOYMENT	LOBBIED FOR
Linda Daschle	FAA Deputy Administrator	American
George Mitchell	Senate Majority Leader, 1989–1995	Northwest
Ken Duberstein	Chief of Staff to Ronald Reagan	Northwest
Bob Packwood	Republican Senator, 1969–1995	United
Wendell Ford	Democratic Senator, 1974–1998	Delta
Harold Ickes	Deputy Chief of Staff to Bill Clinton	United
William Coleman	Secretary, DOT, Ford Administration	US Airways
Patrick Murphy	Deputy Assistant to DOT Secretary	Northwest
William Ris, Jr.	Counsel, Senate Aviation Subcommittee	Continental
Mark Gerchick	Deputy Assistant to DOT Secretary	Northwest

[2] "The Revolving Door," *Miami Herald*, November 11, 2001.

Before 9/11, the FAA was pressured by Congress to go easy on airlines and airports for security lapses, because Congress itself was pressured by lobbyists like Mrs. Daschle and others who represent airlines focused on profits and not "inconveniences" like security. What emerged was a system that resembled cotton candy: 90% sugar and 10% air. When, for example, a checkpoint screener would fail to discover an FAA-approved test object put through by an FAA special agent, the airline would occasionally receive a fine. These fines would accumulate over a period of months or years and finally be negotiated down to pennies on the dollar at special administrative hearings in Washington or other regional FAA offices. The screening company, who was contracted by the airline, would be instructed to fire the offending worker. In most cases, the worker would be rehired shortly thereafter. The blame for the breech would be fixed on the FAA's poor security standards and the screening company's lack of enforcement. The airlines skated every time. And it was the industry's lobbyists who made sure this pattern was allowed to continue.[3]

In 1990, in the wake of the Pan Am 103 explosion over Lockerbie, Scotland, President George H. W. Bush ordered a Presidential Commission on Aviation Security and Terrorism. It concluded its report by saying:

> The U.S. civil aviation security system is seriously flawed and has failed to provide the proper level of protection for the traveling public. This system needs major reform. Rhetoric is no substitute for strong, effective action.[4]

As a result of the commission's findings, a few brave Congressmen sought to impose a 10-year criminal background check on all employees at the nation's airports. This measure was strongly opposed by the airlines on the grounds it wasn't necessary and it would raise security costs to the point that it would ultimately increase passenger fares and hurt the industry.

Another example of how the FAA had its power expropriated by the airline industry via Congressional pressure was the manner in which the industry reacted to the recommendations made by the Gore Commission. On July 25, 1996, shortly after the crash of TWA flight 800, President Clinton asked Vice President Gore to chair a commission on improving air transportation safety and security. As a result, the White House Commission on Aviation Safety and Security, commonly known as the Gore Commission, conducted

---

[3] Andrew R. Thomas, *Aviation Insecurity: The New Challenges of Air Travel* (Amherst, NY: Prometheus, 2003).

[4] The Bush Commission's final report is widely available online. One source is www.globalsecurity.org/security/library/congress/1990_cr/h900521-terror.htm.

an in-depth analysis of the U.S. commercial airlines safeguards against terrorist attacks. In its final report, the Gore Commission found that security measures used by U.S. airlines needed to be drastically improved—the same conclusion the previous federal commission reached six years earlier.

> *The federal government should consider aviation security as a national security issue and provide substantial funding for capital improvements. The Commission believes that terrorist attacks on civil aviation are directed at the United States, and that there should be an ongoing federal commitment to reducing the threats that they pose.*[5]

However, of the 50 recommendations made by the Commission, nearly all were eventually watered down, delayed, or simply never considered by the FAA. On September 5, 1996, the Commission announced its preliminary findings and recommendations at a press conference held by Al Gore. Almost immediately, the airlines began a vigorous lobbying campaign aimed at the White House. Two weeks later, Chairman Gore retreated from the preliminary report in a letter to Carol Hallett, president of the industry's trade group, the Air Transport Association, in which he said, "I want to make it very clear that it is not the intent of this administration or of the commission to create a hardship for the air transportation industry."[6] Gore added that the FAA would develop "a draft test concept ... in full partnership with representatives of the airline industry."[7]

The day after Gore's letter, according to research from the Center for Responsive Politics, TWA donated $40,000 to the Democratic National Committee. By the time of the presidential election six weeks later, other airlines had poured large donations into Democratic Party committees: $265,000 from American Airlines, $120,000 from Delta Air Lines, $115,000 from United Air Lines, $87,000 from Northwest Airlines. In all, the airlines gave the Democratic Party $585,000 in the election's closing weeks. Elaine Kamarck, the Gore aide who worked with the commission, denied that there was any connection between the donations and the commission's decisions. "Everyone was giving us money," she said. "When you're winning, everyone gives."[8]

---

[5] The Gore Commission's final report is widely available online. One source is http://www.fas.org/irp/threat/212fin~1.html.

[6] Walter Johnson and Glen Johnson, "Airlines Fought Security Changes Despite Warnings," *Boston Globe*, September 20, 2001.

[7] Ibid.

[8] Ibid.

Public Citizen, a national public interest organization, analyzed several areas where the FAA's responses to the Commission's proposals reflected the interests of the airlines over better security. Two of the most egregious examples involved the certification of screening companies and employment history, verification, and criminal history records check of all airport and airline employees.[9]

The Gore Commission recommended several ways that the performance of airport screening companies could be improved, including a national job grade structure for screeners, meaningful measures to reduce high turnover rates, rewarding screeners for good performance, and not hiring screening companies on the sole basis of being the lowest bidder. The airlines objected to the proposition on the predictable grounds that it would increase administrative costs significantly. The response to the recommendation from the FAA, in the form of a Proposed Rule, was to maintain the current system of allowing cost, not performance, to be the final determinant as to which screening company would be used by the airline.

With regard to the proposal to conduct criminal background checks of all airport and airline employees, the Gore Commission endorsed the idea and went so far as to suggest the FBI conduct the investigations. In a May 19, 1997 letter, TWA argued that the background checks for their existing employees would only create administrative and financial burdens.

> These employees have had a five-year verification of their employment history. Their continued employment indicates that they have been good employees and do not pose a threat to aviation security. This proposed requirement would not do anything to increase aviation security. It would only add unnecessary costs and paperwork to the industry.[10]

Not surprising, the FAA ignored the Gore Commission's recommendation and nothing was ever done.

Even more disconcerting, several individuals who served on the Gore Commission doubted the genuineness of the recommendations and believed much of the exercise was merely a façade designed to keep market forces in control. One such person was Victoria Cummock, who lost her husband

---

[9] For a complete version of the report "Delay, Dilute, and Discard: How the Airline Industry and the FAA Have Stymied Aviation Security Recommendations", visit Public Citizen's web site at www.citizen.org.

[10] Written comments from TWA before the U.S. Department of Transportation, Federal Aviation Administration, Matter of Notice of Proposed Rulemaking on Employment History Verification and Criminal Records Check contained in the Docket No. FAA 1997-28859, May 19, 1997.

John on Pan Am 103. After the final draft was produced, she stated in a letter to the Vice President:

> *I register my dissent with the final report...Sadly, the overall emphasis of the recommendations reflects a clear commitment to the enhancement of aviation at the expense of the Commission's mandate of enhancing aviation safety and security...I can not sign a report that blatantly allows the American flying public to be regularly placed at unnecessary risk.[11]*

The broader outcome resulting from the marginalization of the FAA as a regulatory body was a disoriented, fragmented, and highly inefficient agency. A culture of compromise festered within the organization for years and came to permeate every level of it. Although isolated pockets of dedicated employees existed throughout the FAA, the majority of the leadership throughout the agency's history was devoted to making things as easy as possible for the airlines. Even on the rare occasion when the FAA pushed back, the airlines were almost always able to leverage their influence both inside and outside of the agency to get what they wanted. As a result, FAA security policy was treated more as a political issue than a mandated responsibility.

The intimate relationship between FAA management and the airlines may be best expressed in the fact that three of the more recent heads of the agency have come directly from the industry. David Hinson, who was in charge of the FAA from 1993 to 1996, was the founder and chief executive of Midway Airlines before joining the agency. The previously mentioned Linda Daschle worked for the Air Transport Association as a lobbyist before joining the FAA as deputy administrator from 1993 to 1996. She served briefly as the acting administrator in parts of 1996 and 1997. Now once again through the revolving door, she is presently back to lobbying for the airlines and for the company that is currently supplying the L-3 baggage screening machines to the Transportation Security Administration. Also, T. Allan McArtor was a top executive at Federal Express both before and after he served as FAA administrator from 1987 to 1989.

In 1996, in response to the obvious long-term negative results stemming from the "Dual Mandate," Congress created new legislation that eliminated some of the language from the original 1958 bill. The FAA Reauthorization Act under Title IV eliminated the word "promotion" and inserted in its

---

[11] Letter from Victoria Cummock, Commissioner, White House Commission on Aviation Safety and Security to Vice President Al Gore, Chairman, White House Commission on Aviation Safety and Security.

place "assigning, maintaining, and enhancing safety and security as the highest priorities in air commerce." Surely, Congress knew all wasn't well with the FAA to have made this adjustment in language. Yet, despite the change in the mission of the FAA, the dysfunctional culture remained. The airlines continued to press their interests and the FAA, for the most part, deferred.

9/11 and the Aviation Security Breakdown

Commercial aviation was used in the 9/11 attacks precisely because of specific defects that existed within the security system—defects that were principally created by the FAA's coziness with the industry. These failings, many of which have received little or no attention at all, literally and figuratively opened the door for the terrorists to do what they did. The warning signs were there for those in charge. They were plain to see, no question about it. However, despite red flags flying everywhere, those entrusted to run aviation security in this country prior to 9/11 dropped the ball.

It's now known that the 9/11 hijackers were casing airports in the weeks prior to the attacks and taking test runs on flights to better pinpoint the weaknesses within the system. Law enforcement officials suggest that the evidence reveals "the hijackers were quiet, studious, calculating, and thorough" in their operation and did so without raising suspicion.[12] In a speech in early May 2002, FBI director Robert Mueller echoed those comments when he said, "The September 11 terrorists spent a great deal of time and effort figuring out how America works. They knew the ins and outs of our systems."[13]

Although it is believed the hijackers took several flights between 1999 and September 11, 2001, the FBI has nailed down twelve flights that the terrorists took immediately prior to the attacks. The FBI believes the terrorists focused on transcontinental flights with lots of fuel, so they could make the planes flying weapons of mass destruction. Testimony from passengers and flight crew reveal that the hijackers took pictures of the cockpit door and appeared to take notes during flights in May, June, July, and August of 2001.[14]

Janice Shineman, who was traveling through the Boston's Logan Airport on September 9, reported to the FBI after the attacks that she observed Mohammed Atta, the alleged ringleader of the 9/11 hijackers, casing the

---

[12] "FBI: 9/11 Hijackers Cased Airports and Took Test Runs," *USA Today*, May 29, 2002.

[13] Ibid.

[14] Ibid.

terminal where American Airlines Flight 11 was boarded. "He had no brief-case, no luggage. I remember telling my limo driver, 'That man has no business here.' " said Shineman, who first spotted Atta as she stepped out of a limou-sine at the American Airlines gate the morning of her flight to California.[15] Shineman added that she watched the fierce-looking Atta take copious notes on a note card "in what looked like Arabic." He then placed the notes into a red envelope.[16] Given that the 9/11 hijackers were searching and probing for weaknesses in the aviation security regimen, it is incumbent for us to understand what they may have seen and learned.

Open Access to the Cockpit

None of the captains or co-captains of the 9/11 flights reported to air traffic controllers that they were being hijacked. It is therefore logical to assume that the terrorists overtook the cockpits in one of the following manners: by stealth; by sudden and brute force; or by creating a disturbance in the air-craft that would have compelled one of the flight deck members to exit the cockpit to handle the situation, thereby exposing the flight deck to penetra-tion by the hijackers. Remember, had the 9/11 terrorists not been able to get into the cockpit of the airliners, they wouldn't have been able to turn the plane into a flying missile and inflict the damage on the ground that they did.

On at least two of the hijacked flights, communications with the doomed airliners prior to the crashes revealed that flight attendants had been stabbed and killed. On American Flight 11, the first to slam into the World Trade Center, flight attendant Betty Ong called the American reservations desk from a seatback phone. "She said two flight attendants had been stabbed, one was on oxygen," said the manager on duty.[17] On United Flight 175, the second plane to fly into the WTC, the airline reported that one flight attendant had been stabbed and two crewmembers were killed.[18] The most likely reason for the assaults on the flight attendants was that they were each carrying a key to the cockpit door, in compliance with FAA regulations. We can assume, therefore, that the terrorists were quite able to unlock the doors and literally walk into the cockpits.

---

[15] Jennifer Rosinski and Jow Dwinell, "Woman Reflects on Seeing Atta," *Boston Herald*, May 29, 2002.

[16] Ibid.

[17] WorldNetDaily.com/Paul Sperry, "Terrorists Slit Throats of 2 AA Stewardesses," http://www.wnd.com/?pageId=10818, September 11, 2001.

[18] This information is taken from the FAA's Executive Summary of September 11, 2001. A com-plete copy of this document is included in the Appendix of this book.

FAA Order Number 8400.10, dated January 7, 1997, responded to a National Transportation Safety Board recommendation, which asked the FAA to require each flight attendant to have a cockpit key in his/her possession at all times while on duty. Remarkably, this is what the order said, in the FAA's own words:

> During a recent accident, the pilots received information that they had an engine fire when the right engine fire warning light illuminated... Because of the need for a flight attendant to retrieve a cockpit key from its assigned storage area before being able to unlock the cockpit door, the Safety Board is concerned that having only one cockpit key available and stored in a prearranged area may not allow a key to be readily accessible to all flight attendants in an emergency. Therefore, the Safety Board believes that the FAA should require that each flight attendant have a cockpit key in his/her possession at all times, while on duty.

To justify their decision, Title 14 of the Code of Federal Regulations (14 CFR) part 121, section 121.313(g) was cited. It stipulated that there must be a key for each door that separates a passenger compartment from another compartment that has emergency exit provisions. The key must be readily available for each crewmember. In addition, 14 CFR part 121, section 121.587, stipulates that the cockpit door must be locked during flight. "Therefore, air carriers should ensure that each flight attendant has a cockpit key in his/her possession during the performance of duties in flight."

Failure to Address the Growing Air Rage Problem

For the ten years prior to 9/11, not a single commercial aircraft was hijacked in the United States. For nearly a generation, disturbances perpetrated by disruptive passengers were widely viewed as the greatest threat to cabin security. For example, in calendar year 2000, internal FAA research revealed that more than 10,000 cases of "air rage"—an abusive, abnormal, or aberrant act—took place during calendar year 2000. Nevertheless, despite the scope and magnitude of the problem, nothing of consequence was ever done. In 2000, only 266 cases of disruptive behavior, less than 3% of all incidents, were ever prosecuted.[19]

---

[19] At the risk of appearing arrogant, one of the most definitive works on the problem of air rage is my book *Air Rage: Crisis in the Skies* (Amherst, NY: Prometheus Books, 2001).

After United Flight 175 was hijacked, a dispatcher sitting at the transcontinental desk at United's operation center in Chicago, who had been assigned to follow both flights 175 and 93 as well as 14 other planes, sent an electronic text message out to the airliners that read "Beware, cockpit intrusion."[20] On the morning of September 11, 2001, such a message would almost certainly been interpreted by the pilot of a domestic flight as an air rage incident, not a hijacking. On United Flight 93, the last of the four planes to be hijacked, the pilots received the message and typed a one-word reply: "Confirmed." The plane was taken over by four terrorists a few minutes later.[21]

In the 24 months prior to September 11, 2001, some 30 cases were recorded of passengers either completely or partially entering the cockpit of a commercial carrier. In one of the more publicized cases, on a Southwest flight from Las Vegas to Salt Lake City in August 2000, a 19 year-old passenger rushed and entered the cockpit twice before other passengers subdued him. He eventually died from suffocation and the death was ruled a homicide. Nevertheless, the U.S. Attorney in Salt Lake City did not file charges against the passengers because he felt there was no criminal conduct involved.[22]

On March 16, 2000, during an Alaska Airlines flight from Mexico to San Francisco, a male passenger began babbling incoherently, wandering from seat to seat, and stripping off his clothes. His agitation increased, passengers said, until he broke into the cockpit, threatened the pilots, and grabbed for the controls. The pilot momentarily lost control of the jet as the co-pilot fended off the 6-foot-2, 250-pound intruder with an axe. Some of the 41 passengers aboard tackled and eventually restrained him.

In one of the more frightening cockpit intrusion incidents in December 2000, a deranged passenger broke into the cockpit of a British Airways jumbo jet traveling from London to Nairobi and grabbed the controls, sending the plane plummeting toward the ground before the crew regained control. According to statements from passengers and crew, the man, after barging into the cockpit, disengaged the autopilot, and sent the plane hurtling into a 10,000 foot dive. The crew struggled with the man, sending the plane into a second dive. Many of the 379 passengers aboard the Boeing 747-400 screamed and prayed as they were jolted out of their early morning slumber. For more than two minutes, passengers believed they were going to die as

---

[20] Matthew Wald, "'We Have Some Planes', Hijacker Told Controller," *New York Times*, October 16, 2001.

[21] Ibid.

[22] This and the other accounts of air rage depicted here are in my book *Air Rage: Crisis in the Skies* (Amherst, NY: Prometheus Books, 2001).

the plane continued to plummet. Finally, after what must have seemed like an eternity, first class passengers and flight crew overpowered the man. During the melee, the intruder bit the ear of the captain and injured four other passengers and a crew member. The first officer was eventually able to get the man out of the cockpit while the reserve officer was able to fly the aircraft. Aviation experts believe that had the incident raged on for another four or five seconds, the co-pilot would not have been able to regain control of the plane because the aircraft was nearly on its back. The results of the medical examinations conducted on the passenger showed that the 27-year old Kenyan was mentally disturbed. Passengers said they saw the perpetrator wandering around one section of the plane for about 30 minutes before he made his way toward the cockpit and burst in, lunging for the controls.

One hour into a February 2001 flight from Miami to New York, a young couple sitting in coach class calmly asked the flight attendant if they could move into the two empty seats in the first-class section because "they believed the elderly woman sitting in the aisle next them was trying to kill them." The attendant, believing they were joking, politely said "No" and continued serving drinks. At this point, a seemingly normal trip became a near-disaster. The girlfriend, incredulous that she was denied an upgrade, became enraged. Screaming obscenities at the top of her lungs, she jumped up from her seat and made a mad dash, on her knees, for first-class.

Following his girlfriend's lead, the man stood up and announced to everyone that the overhead compartments were filled with machine guns and that she was carrying a bomb. As his girlfriend continued to run towards the front of the plane, the boyfriend grabbed two coffeepots and yelled, "These are my weapons!" as he threw coffee on a flight attendant and burned her. Reaching first-class, the man kicked a hole in the cockpit door and the woman grabbed the emergency exit handle shouting, "We're taking this plane down!" Fortunately, four male passengers tackled the boyfriend before he could do anything else, beating him unconscious, while two other flight attendants subdued the woman and then sat on her until the flight could be diverted to Atlanta. Upon arrival, the two were sent to a hospital for observation. They were released after it was discovered that they were both under psychiatric evaluation in their hometown. Their family doctor had ordered them to take their medication and stay within 5 miles of their residence. Unfortunately, they had the urge to travel and acted upon it.

Whether drunk, mentally ill, or under the influence of narcotics, disruptive passengers educated the 9/11 hijackers how easy it was to storm the cockpit of an aircraft. Imagine how simple it could have been for four or five well-motivated and calculating terrorists to get in. And, despite the heightened security measures following 9/11, seven incidents involving disruptive passengers completely or partially entering a cockpit took place in the six months *after* the attacks.

These cockpit intrusions would not have been possible, however, had the structure of the door been reinforced. Instead, to ensure easy egress from the flight deck in the case of an emergency, cockpit doors were designed to be weak. A normal-sized man with a karate kick or a shoulder shove could have broken down a 9/11 cockpit door without too much exertion. Because of the cost to the airlines of reinforcing the cockpit doors of 8,000 commercial airliners, the FAA failed to do anything about the problem. In hearings on Capitol Hill in early 2001, Senator John McCain and other lawmakers stressed airline delays, missed flights, and lost baggage, and largely overlooked security problems, although FAA agents, consumer groups, and flight attendants had clamored for years for stronger cockpit doors, which were implemented only after 9/11.

Although the FAA wasn't doing anything to address the rising tide of air rage, airlines had formulated policies that created glaring security vulnerabilities on 9/11. In the event of a disruptive incident in the cabin that appeared to be escalating, pilots were encouraged by the airlines to intervene personally to de-escalate the situation. Rather than divert the flight to the nearest airport where law enforcement officials could handle the situation, pilots were instructed to exit the cockpit and confront the disruptive passenger head on.

Lax Screening Protocols

Incredibly, nine of the hijackers were selected for special security screenings the morning of 9/11. Six were chosen for extra security by a computerized screening system. Two others were singled out because of irregularities with their documents. And one was listed on ticket documents as traveling with one of the hijackers with questionable identification.[23] Yet, in the end, they were all allowed to later board their flights.

On 9/11, according to FAA security protocols, passengers selected for further evaluation were only to have their *checked* luggage further swept for explosives or unauthorized weapons. The passenger's carry-on bag and their person were not to be more fully examined. And, as only a couple of the terrorists actually had checked bags, there was no security protocol in place

---

[23] Dan Eggen, "Airports Screened Nine of September 11 Hijackers," *Washington Post*, March 2, 2002, p. A11.

to detect the box cutters and other possible weapons they were carrying with them. Had a security protocol requiring more intensive examination of *all* luggage—both carry-ons and checked bags—of a selected passenger existed, as well as clothing, it is more than likely that the discovery of several young Arab men carrying box cutters who had purchased one-way, first class tickets with cash would have thrown up a red flag. Unfortunately, we'll never know.

9/11 and the Intelligence Breakdown

In the weeks before September 11, the Bush Administration was made very much aware of a number of warnings that pointed to an attack on the United States by members of Al Qaeda, possibly using commercial aviation as the *modus operandi*. In early June 2001, when the Group of Eight met for their annual meeting in Genoa, Italy, the government of Egypt sent a warning to the Bush Administration about a possible suicide hijacker. In an interview with the French newspaper *Le Figaro*, Egyptian President Hosni Mubarak said he had uncovered a video where Osama Bin Laden "spoke of assassinating President Bush and other heads of state in Genoa... using an airplane stuffed with explosives."[24] To respond to this potential threat, anti-aircraft missile batteries were placed around the city during the summit.

On June 28, National Security Adviser Condoleezza Rice received an intelligence summary warning that a significant Al Qaeda attack in the near future was "highly likely." One-week later, on July 5, National Security Council terrorism chief, Richard Clarke, convened a White House meeting of the Counterterrorism Security Group (CSG). Later that same day, Clarke met with National Security Advisor Rice and Bush Chief of Staff Andrew Card. Following that meeting, another CSG session was held, which this time included representatives from the Federal Aviation Administration, FBI, and Immigration and Naturalization Service. Clarke told them that "something spectacular is going to happen."[25]

On July 18, the FAA warned the airlines to exercise the highest level of caution. Thirteen days later, on July 31, the FAA advised the airlines that terrorists were planning and training for hijackings. On August 17, the INS detained Zacharias Moussaoui for suspicious activity at a Minnesota flight

---

[24] David Sanger, "Two Leaders Tell of Plot to Kill Bush in Genoa," *New York Times*, September 26, 2001.

[25] Michael Isikoff and David Klaidman, "The Hijackers We Let Escape", *Newsweek*, June 10, 2002.

school; he was later identified as the 20th hijacker for the 9/11 attacks. On September 4, a week before the attacks, the FBI told the FAA of Moussaoui's arrest. However, the FAA did not alert the airlines.

The government explanations in the days and months following the attacks were predictable. On September 17, 2001, recently appointed FBI Director Robert Mueller insisted his agency "had no warning signs" of the previous week's attacks. When asked by a reporter at a news conference whether the federal government was ever anticipating a 9/11 type attack, Ari Fleischer, White House spokesperson, said, "I don't think this should come as any surprise to anybody," speaking of the warnings given to President Bush months before the attacks. "But the president did not—not receive information about the use of airplanes as missiles by suicide bombers. This was a new type of attack that was not foreseen."[26]

In a press conference the next day at the White House, National Security Advisor Rice concurred. "The government did everything that it could—in a period in which the information was very generalized, in which there was nothing specific in which to react—and had this president known of something more specific or known that a plane was going to be used as a missile, he would have acted on it."[27] With all due respect to Mr. Fleischer and Dr. Rice, the administration for whom they were working was either incredibly inexperienced or spinning their version of the truth. The fact is, enough of the dots were already connected so that a definable picture was beginning to come forth.

Still, to be fair, knowing exactly when and where terrorists will strike was and remains to the present day quite difficult to determine. The ease of movement the terrorists enjoyed both inside and outside of the U.S. prior to 9/11 made it challenging for even the best analyst to accurately predict their plans and intentions. So, apparently, was keeping track of two of the hijackers who eventually boarded American Airlines Flight 77 and crashed it into the Pentagon. According to published reports, the CIA knew Nawaf Alhazmi and Khalid Almihdhar were in the United States and that they were connected to Al Qaeda. For nearly 21 months after they were identified by the CIA as terrorists, Alhazmi and Almihdhar lived openly in the United States, using their real names, getting driver's licenses, opening bank accounts, and attending flight schools.[28]

---

[26] Ibid.

[27] Ibid.

[28] Ibid.

Incredibly, the CIA did nothing with the information—neither notifying the FBI, which could have tracked down the two men, nor the INS, which could have turned them away at the border. Almihdhar, remarkably, was able to obtain a multiple-entry visa from the U.S. Embassy in Saudi Arabia that allowed him to enter and leave the United States at will. When Almihdhar's visa expired, the State Department, not knowing any better, issued him a new one in July 2001, even though the CIA had linked him to one of the suspected bombers of the USS Cole in Yemen in October 2000.[29]

To blame only the Bush Administration for the intelligence failures would be disingenuous, however. The Clinton Administration also missed much of what was so obvious. With the exception of Rice, it is a sad fact that President Bush's intelligence team was composed almost entirely of Clinton administration holdovers or career bureaucrats promoted by these same holdovers. There were no transition or changes in personnel at CIA when the new administration took office in 2001. Likewise at the FBI, Louis Freeh and his handpicked deputies were kept on with no changes after Bush's inauguration in January.

Not A Novel Idea

The notion of a suicidal hijacker turning an aircraft into a flying missile is not a novel idea. For those who claimed they couldn't have imagined such a scenario, they only needed to look at how such an act had been actually been threatened or accomplished in the past.

In December 1994, the Armed Islamic Group hijacked an Air France flight from Algiers. The hijackers ordered the plane flown to Marseilles, in the south of France, where it landed. They ordered authorities to load an additional 27 tons of aviation fuel for a journey to Paris, although the trip required only about one-third that amount. The hijackers aim was to crash the plane into the Eiffel Tower. While still on the ground in Marseilles, commandos from French Special Forces stormed the plane.[30]

In 1995, the FBI was warned of a terrorist plot to hijack several commercial airliners and slam them into the Pentagon and the CIA. In January of that year, a fire in the Manila apartment building of Abdul Murad and Ramzi Yousef led Philippine investigators to uncover a plot to plant timed explosive devices on several U.S. airliners. The apartment, in which police found

---

[29] Ibid.

[30] Ibid.

contained bomb-making equipment, led them to Murad, who was captured in Manila. Yousef was out of the country at the time. During intense and of-ten brutal interrogations by Philippine authorities, Murad told of detailed plans to simultaneously blow up several planes over the Pacific Ocean while he and another suicide hijacker could each carry out a kamikaze suicide at-tack on the CIA and Pentagon, respectively.[31]

Later that same year, Yousef, the ringleader of the first World Trade Cen-ter bombing in 1993, was arrested in Pakistan and turned over to the United States. On his flight back to the U.S. for trial, Yousef reportedly told FBI agent Brian Parr and the other agents guarding him that he had narrowly missed several opportunities to blow up a dozen airliners on a single day over the Pacific and carry out a suicidal attack on CIA headquarters in Lan-gley, Virginia.[32] It is still unclear whether this compelling information was ever disseminated among other security agencies.

Before the 1996 Summer Olympics that were held in Atlanta, Georgia, intel-ligence officials at FBI and CIA had identified crop-dusters and suicide flights as potential terrorist weapons and took steps to prevent an attack from the air during the games. Black Hawk helicopters and Customs Service jets were deployed to intercept suspicious aircraft in the skies over Atlanta. Law enforcement agents monitored crop-dusters and fanned out across the re-gion "to make sure nobody hijacked a small aircraft and tried to attack one of the venues," said Woody Johnson, the FBI agent in charge of the Atlanta office at the time.[33]

Beyond the warning from Egypt that was received prior to the G8 summit, several other governments had notified Washington of increased Al Qaeda activity and the rising specter of an attack on the U.S. According to press re-ports in Russia, Russian intelligence notified the CIA during the summer of 2001 that 25 terrorist pilots had been specifically training for suicide mis-sions. In an interview on September 15 with MSNBC, Russian President Vla-dimir Putin confirmed that he had ordered Russian intelligence in August to warn the U.S. government "in the strongest terms" of imminent attacks on airports and government buildings. Earlier in June, the BND, the German in-telligence service, warned the CIA and Israel that Middle Eastern terrorists

---

[31] Doug Struck, "Borderless Network of Terror, Bin Laden Followers Reach Across the Globe," *Washington Post*, September 23, 2001.

[32] Ibid.

[33] Mark Fireman and Judy Pasternak, "Suicide Flights and Crop Dusters Considered Threats at '96 Olympics," *Los Angeles Times*, November 17, 2001.

were "planning to hijack commercial aircraft to use as weapons to attack important symbols of American and Israeli culture."[34]

A Prescient Sage Emerges

A staunch critic of the government's lack of action in the face of warning lights going off everywhere was Brian Sullivan, a retired U.S. Army Military Police Lieutenant Colonel and former FAA Civil Aviation Security Specialist for the New England Region. Sullivan, who left the FAA in January 2001, set out after his departure to expose what he called "the façade of aviation security that existed at Logan prior to the terrorist attacks."[35]

To prove his point, Sullivan contacted Deborah Sherman, an investigative reporter with WFXT television in Boston. In April of 2001, Sherman, with the help of Steve Elson, another retired FAA agent, conducted tests at Logan's screening checkpoints. On May 6, the broadcast aired and revealed that reporters were able to get items that should have been detected and resolved past screeners at Logan 11 out of 12 times. One such example was a 6¾-inch knife reporters were able to pass through in a belly pack that was never discovered. In addition, reporters were able to glean combinations to airport terminal doors, which gave them unfettered access to parked aircraft and cargo.

In what would come to be a prophetic letter (Figure 6-1) to Massachusetts Senator John Kerry dated May 7, 2001, the day after the broadcast, Brian Sullivan wrote:

> With the concept of Jihad, do you think it would be difficult for a determined terrorist to get on a plane and destroy himself and all other passengers? Think what the result would be of a coordinated attack that took down several domestic flights on the same day. Considering the current threats, it is almost likely. [36]

---

[34] Ibid.

[35] Conversation with author, June 2002.

[36] A complete copy of this document is included in the Appendix of this book

22 Carolyn Drive
Plymouth, MA 02360

May 7, 2001

The Honorable John F. Kerry
304 Russell Senate Office Building
Washington, DC 20510

Dear Senator Kerry,

There was a very disturbing investigative report last night (Sunday evening May 6) on Channel 25 FOX News at 10PM regarding airport security. Although the report focused on Logan Airport and TF Green in Rhode Island, as a recently retired FAA Special Agent, I know this is a national problem, not one simply unique to New England Region. I've asked my friend Steve Elson, another former FAA Special Agent, to forward a video copy of the report to you. Both of us are willing to testify before Congress should the need arise and we are both committed to doing whatever is necessary to improving our aviation security system. We are hopeful that you would show the video to your peers, Senator McCain and members of any House committee dealing with aviation security.

The FAA does everything it can to prevent news reports of this nature under the guise of it being a public safety issue, which should not be given a public forum. Unfortunately, this report once again demonstrated what every FAA line agent already knows, the airport passenger screening system simply doesn't work as intended. The FAA would prefer to continue to promulgate a façade of security, than to honestly assess the system. Management knows how ineffective the current system is, but continues to tell Congress that our airport screening is an effective deterrent.

FAA officials point to a 95+% success rate of FAA screening checkpoint tests, particularly when reassuring the flying public and Congress. They do this even though they know that every time a Red Team, or news reporter in this instance, tests the system, the exact opposite occurs with a failure rate of 95+%. The difference is realistic testing versus tests designed to avoid enforcement litigation problems with the airlines. It is a clear example of self fulfilling prophecy, whereby the tests are designed to produce a desired outcome, rather than to truly reflect the status of aviation security.

FAA management will point to a decline in incidents of hijacking since the system was put into effect in the '70s. My question is, "Have they kept up with the times?" Do you see a horde of Cuban exiles just waiting to commit air piracy to return to Havana? Or, has the threat become more refined over the years? I've stood along the Potomac and watched our big air ships fly in low and slow along the river. What protection is there against a rogue terrorist with a Stinger missile? While the FAA has focused on screening for handguns, new threats have emerged, such as chemical and biological weapons. Do you really think a screener could detect a bottle of liquid explosive, small battery and detonator in your carry on baggage? And with the concept of Jihad, do you think it would be difficult for a determined terrorist to get on a plane and destroy himself and all other passengers? The answers to these questions are obvious.

The FAA was dubbed "The Tombstone Agency" by Mary Schiavo, the former DOT OIG. The reason is that the agency never seems to act until there has been an air tragedy. Think for a moment how vital the air transportation industry is to our overall economic well being as a nation. Think what the result would be of a coordinated attack which took down several domestic flights on the same day. The problem is that with our current screening system, this is more than possible. Given time, considering current threats, and it is almost likely. We don't have to wait for a tragedy to occur to act. There are simple, cost effective means to improve the system now.

The DOT OIG has become an ineffective overseer of the FAA, particularly since Mary Schiavo's departure. Scathing reports have been developed on airport/airline security and FAA facility security. Still, the culture continues to perpetuate itself and managers have been promoted up the chain, despite the fact that they've supported this façade of security and abused line agents who dare to speak the truth. The answer here is not to fire a few hapless low paid screeners or continue to issue meaningless fines against the airlines. The answer is to change the prevailing culture within Civil Aviation Security at the FAA from one concerned with continuing to support the façade, to one committed to protecting the traveling public. Let our agents do their job. Don't stifle initiative and independent thought and observations. Don't continue to silence those who refuse to buy the party line and actually attempt to reveal the façade.

It is time for the truth to be known, before an incident occurs. It is not in the best interests of public safety to continue this façade of security. Hopefully, FOX 25 will distribute this report to all its national affiliates and encourage similar testing. National TV news magazines could also help bring focus. Perhaps we can force a public forum where line agents could testify before Congress and finally secure an honest assessment of aviation security, as well as some positive change.

Thank you,

Brian F. Sullivan
FAA Spec Agent (Ret)
508-224-7775

Figure 6-1. Brian Sullivan's letter to Senator John Kerry.

Sullivan further asked Kerry not to send his letter or a copy of the television report to the Department of Transportation's Office of Inspector General (DOT OIG). Sullivan believed the DOT OIG was compromised. Instead, Sullivan requested Kerry contact the General Accounting Office:

> The answer here is not to fire a few hapless low-paid screeners or continue to issue meaningless fines against the airlines. The answer is to change the prevailing culture within Civil Aviation Security at the FAA from one concerned with continuing to support the façade, to one committed to protecting the traveling public.

Unfortunately, against Sullivan's wishes, Senator Kerry sent his letter and videotape to the Department of Transportation. Not surprisingly, nothing happened, until 118 days later when American Flight 11 departed at 7:59 a.m. from Boston's Logan International for Los Angeles from Gate 26 in Terminal B with 92 people on board. Fifteen minutes later, United Flight 175, also bound for the west coast, departed Logan from Gate 19 in Terminal C with 65 people on board. Less than three hours later, the World Trade Center in New York would be a smoldering ruin and nearly 3,000 innocent people would be dead.

JOHN F. KERRY
MASSACHUSETTS

United States Senate
WASHINGTON, DC 20510-2102

COMMITTEES
COMMERCE, SCIENCE,
AND TRANSPORTATION
FINANCE
FOREIGN RELATIONS
SMALL BUSINESS

July 24, 2001

Mr. Brian F. Sullivan
22 Carolyn Drive
Plymouth, Massachusetts 02360-1619

Dear Mr. Sullivan:

Thank you for contacting me regarding your work on civil aviation security issues. I appreciate hearing from you.

I have forwarded your tape of WFXT-25's recent report on airport security to the Department of Transportation's Office of the Inspector General (OIG). My staff has requested that the OIG respond to me after viewing the tape.

Thank you again for bringing this matter to my attention. Please do not hesitate to contact me further on this or any issue.

Sincerely,

John F. Kerry
United States Senator

JFK/jdwb

PLEASE RESPOND TO

☐ 304 RUSSELL SENATE OFFICE BUILDING
WASHINGTON, DC 20510
(202) 224-2742

☐ ONE BOWDOIN SQUARE
10TH FLOOR
BOSTON, MA 02114
(617) 565-8519

☐ 222 MILLIKEN PLACE
SUITE 311
FALL RIVER, MA 02722
(508) 677-0522

☐ ONE FINANCIAL PLAZA
12TH FLOOR
SPRINGFIELD, MA 01103
(413) 785-4610

☐ 90 MADISON PLACE
SUITE 206
WORCESTER, MA 01608
(508) 831-7880

email john_kerry@kerry.senate.gov
www.kerry.senate.gov

PRINTED ON RECYCLED PAPER

Figure 6-2. Senator John Kerry's letter to Brian Sullivan.

The Creation of the TSA

By every measurable standard, the federal government's system in place to prevent attacks against civil aviation failed miserably on September 11, 2001. The attacks simply weren't that hard to pull off. The hijackings and ground attacks were not merely a failure of imagination. They were, in fact, the product of a compromised system that virtually guaranteed the terrorist's success once they boarded the four planes. The only tool the terrorists really needed was the will to execute the plan. Everything else was provided to them by the same system being attacked.

From the moments the World Trade Center towers collapsed, the nation was obsessed with preventing another suicide hijacking. Cockpit doors were reinforced—finally, but too late. National guardsmen were stationed at airports around the country. Military jets patrolled the skies, at-the-ready to shoot down any hijacked plane. Fears about suspicious behavior—whatever that meant—resulted in dozens of terminal evacuations and di-verted landings.

The 9/11 attacks created a crisis of confidence in the air transport system. The fallout was evident everywhere. Tourists cancelled vacation plans. Cor-porations put a halt on much of their employees' travel schedules. The number of empty airline seats, rental cars, hotel rooms, and theme parks skyrocketed. President George W. Bush, in a defining moment, asked Americans to demonstrate their patriotism by taking a vacation; going to Disney World; running up their credit cards; and, proving to the terrorists that "we won't be defeated" (a bit different than the call 60 years earlier from the commander-in-chief after the surprise at Pearl Harbor, where shared sacrifice became the national mantra). Still, despite Bush's pleadings, people stayed home in droves, not just in America, but also around the world. Something needed to be done immediately to jump-start the system.

The Travel Industry Association spent a small fortune on patriotic adver-tisements, blazing images across American television sets, radio stations, and billboards. These ads echoed the President's admonition that Americans had a responsibility as good citizens to hit the road and prove the American way of life was stronger than Al-Qaeda's actions. In response to this *faux* call of duty, Americans found themselves asking: "How about the duty of the air-line industry and the federal government to fix their problems?"

There was no one who believed the FAA was capable of handling the re-sponsibility of aviation security anymore. Conventional wisdom began to take hold that the FAA was too close to the industry to implement the kind of security changes necessary to reassure a skittish flying public. Many in Congress, who a few days earlier had been some of the most ardent supporters of the cozy FAA/industry "partnership," now began to look for a new way of securing the nation's air transport system.

Max Cleland, a Georgia Democrat and member of the Senate Commerce, Science, and Transportation Committee, began to reflect the mood of many on Capitol Hill after the attacks when he said, "What happened is we dumbed down the security system because an airline is going to want to cut costs, specifically when we have a downturn in the economy and they are fighting for their lives."[37] Time was of the essence. Again, Senator Cleland: "We've got to move fast on this, because the airlines are bleeding. Unless they get 65 percent capacity in that cabin, they don't make any money. So, security is number one in a series of confidence-building measures that will bring people back to fly."[38]

Further, the scope and magnitude of the 9/11 attacks spoke to the need to look at aviation security as more than a singular activity confined to one industry. Airports and airliners were now seen by many as the frontlines in a new "war on terror." Aviation security, the argument held, had now become a key of any country's overall national security.

This view was particularly put forth by the airlines, which saw an opportunity to finally offload all of the hassle and costs they had been dealing with concerning aviation security since the 1970s. Carol Hallett, then president of the Air Transport Association, the industry's trade and lobbying group, hyperbolically declared, "Today, airport security is no longer a passenger issue. It is an issue of national security. Our planes were used as missiles of mass destruction. And, unless the national security of America is maintained by the government and not just airlines and their passengers, the terrorists will win!"[39]

To be fair, the American public also wanted action. A Gallup poll conducted just days before the attacks asked Americans whether the federal government was trying to do too many things that should be left to individuals and businesses, or whether it should do more to solve the country's problems. Fifty-five percent thought the government was doing too much, compared

---

[37] CNN/Mike Fish, "Airport Security: A System Driven by the Minimum Wage," http://www.cnn.com/SPECIALS/2001/trade.center/flight.risk/stories/part1.mainbar.html.

[38] Ibid.

[39] Remarks of Carol B. Hallett, president of the Air Transport Association, to the TIA Marketing Outlook Forum 2001, Atlanta, Georgia, October 2, 2001.

with 36 percent who thought it should do more. When the same poll was repeated a few weeks after the 9/11 attacks, the results flipped: 41 percent thought the government was doing too much, while 51 percent believed it should do more to solve the country's problems.[40]

Specific to aviation security, in a *Newsweek* survey just after the attacks, when asked what would be "very effective" in preventing similar terrorist attacks, the public rated "more security at airports" (76 percent) and in-flight precautions like air marshals and locked cockpit doors (75 percent) ahead of military strikes (49 percent) and killing suspected terrorist leaders (44 percent).[41]

Across the country it was becoming evident that the government's assumption of a stronger role in aviation security would be a crucial step that would go far in resolving public concerns over the safety of the system. The federalization of the aviation security system seemed a foregone conclusion. The only real debate seemed to be about how that system would look under full government control.

The Aviation and Transportation Security Act

President Bush signed the legislation that took away the FAA's aviation security role and gave it to the newly formed Transportation Security Administration (TSA) on November 19, 2001. Thus, in a little more than two months, the entire way that aviation security would now be done in America was supposed to be inexorably changed—a remarkable achievement in the normally gridlocked Capitol. In his remarks immediately after signing the Aviation and Transportation Security Act (ATSA), the president sounded supremely confident in government's ability to build confidence back in the air transport system:

> For the first time, aviation security will become a direct federal responsibility....Security comes first. The federal government will set high standards, and we will enforce them. A proud industry has been hit hard. But this nation has seen the dedication and spirit of our pilots and flight crews, and the hundreds of thousands of hard-working people who keep

---

[40] Susan E. Dudley, "Regulation, Post-9/11," *National Review*, March 26, 2002.

[41] "Public Optimism Growing in War on Terror," http://www.washingtonpost.com/wp-srv/politics/polls/vault/stories/data122101.htm.

America flying. We know they will endure. I'm confident this industry will grow and prosper.[42]

The new legislation made the TSA responsible for day-to-day security screening operations for passenger air transportation. That responsibility included hiring, training, testing, deploying, or arranging for federal security screeners, federal security personnel, federal law enforcement officers, and federal security managers at all U.S. airports. The TSA was also mandated to research, develop, and deploy security equipment and programs at U.S. airports, coordinate transportation security efforts with federal and state agencies, and deal with threats to transportation. To the glee of the airlines, the costs for all of this would not be borne by the industry. Instead, under the legislation, the TSA was to impose a uniform fee on passenger beginning February 1, 2002. A corresponding fee on both U.S. and foreign air carriers was to be assessed based on their calendar year 2000 costs for screening passengers and property. Of course, that was just simply passed on to passengers in the form of higher fares.

A new beginning was at hand. Unfortunately, it would be realized very quickly that the creation of the TSA was a woefully horrible idea. Even more disconcerting, the TSA is now one of the biggest threats to the industry's sustainability moving forward.

---

[42] Remarks by President George W. Bush at the signing of the Aviation Security Legislation, Ronald Reagan National Airport, Washington, D.C., November 19, 2001.

Touching Your Junk and Viewing Your Cavity

The Future of Aviation "Security"

"Good security and bad security look a lot like each other, at least on the surface."

—Anonymous

Terrorism, if properly conducted by the terrorists, generates disproportionate feelings of anger, fear, and vulnerability in the population that is attacked. This is what it means to be terrorized. This terrorization leads the population to pressure their government to do things to alleviate their anger, fear, and vulnerability. The bigger the attack, the more pressure on government to *do something*, whether tangibly or symbolically. Of course, feeding all of this is the international media, whose coverage of anything airline-related is way over the top.

The decision to attack Afghanistan in the aftermath of 9/11 was a response by the U.S. government to do something of tangible value in the wake of the attacks. Taking it right to Osama Bin Laden and Al-Qaeda where they lived was almost universally accepted as a rational response, at least initially. On the other hand, it can be argued with hindsight (and I tend to agree) that the creation of the TSA and the new post-9/11 aviation security regime was ultimately much more symbolic in nature.

Here's my thinking: The scope and magnitude of America's air transport system is remarkable. There are about 26,000 take-offs and nearly 2 million passengers screened each day. Think about those numbers for a moment: 26,000 flights and 2 million checkpoint processes every 24 hours, 365 days a year. Israel, who many so-called experts tout as the best example of how to design and implement a well-run aviation security system, has less than that many flights and passenger screenings in a year.

I've been able to estimate that the U.S. at the time of this writing has spent somewhere around $75 billion since 9/11 to deploy the current TSA-led system in this country. What we can't calculate is the cost in passenger frustration and stress the new system has brought on. Further, despite everything that has happened—and not happened—a well-trained terrorist can still devise any number of ways to get explosives or other devices through the system. Whether in shoes, underwear, bras, or toner cartridges, human innovation in the form of terrorist action has been able to beat the system. Why? There is simply no security system in existence—nor will there ever be—that is both dynamic enough to detect and stop terrorists reliably and efficient enough to permit the airline industry to function as it needs to. In short, aviation security is at best an attempt to make passengers *feel* safer, as if the more steps you have to go through (read hassle and stress) will actually comfort you and persuade you that the system is indeed safe. If the security screening process was quick and without any hassle, the logic goes, people would question the safety of the system and likely stay away from flying. The formula is this: the more security activity, the more reassuring it is to the flying public.

As a result, when a terrorist attack against the air transport system is successful—or at least foiled in public—the automatic response from the government has been to ratchet up security measures. When the shoe bomber was stopped in-flight in 2001, the measure of taking off our shoes was implemented. Expensive in manpower? Yes. Time consuming and a hassle? Absolutely. But it is also psychologically comforting for passengers that, despite the costs, we must somehow be better off because our shoes are screened. The same is true with the underwear bomber. The ubiquitous "naked x-ray machines" and intensive pat-downs are direct results of the foiled attack on

Christmas Day 2009 . At the very basic level where most people live, endur-ing these new security measures and the humiliation that goes along with them reassures us that our personal safety, and that of our loved ones, is guaranteed. This speaks to the contradictions that are in everyone and eve-rywhere. The reality, however, is that once we rise above the emotion and look coldly at the system, we see that it is pretty much window dressing and theater—and always will be.

Moving forward, the danger for the airline industry when it comes to secu-rity is that as terrorist innovation continues, and the government predicta-bly responds to what the bad guys do by implementing more measures to reassure travelers, there may well come a point in time when the trade-off no longer makes sense—so passengers will ultimately stay away. That is, se-curity measures will become too invasive and the emotional comfort from them will be lost. In fact, this may already be happening. But before we get there, let's look back—way back—to the origins of commercial air travel.

Early Security Breaches

When most folks are asked what year the first bombing of a commercial air-liner took place, the answers likely fall somewhere between 1950 and 1970. Few people know that on October 10, 1933, a United Airlines flight bound for Chicago exploded over Chesterton, Indiana.

At 6:57 p.m., the Boeing 247 with four passengers and three flight crew-members aboard departed Cleveland and passed over Toledo some 43 min-utes later. At 8:45 p.m., the pilot, Richard Tarrant, of Oak Park, Illinois, ra-dioed from over North Liberty, Indiana, that all was well and he was flying at a cruising altitude of 1,500 feet.

At a little after 9:00 p.m., several residents of this small northwest Indiana town reported hearing and seeing an explosion in the sky. John Tillotson, who lived near where the plane went down, said he was sitting by a window when the plane exploded and he saw it clearly. He believed he heard screams and a woman's voice shouting, "Help! Help! Oh my God."[1] Accord-ing to other witnesses who also observed the first explosion, the plane blew up a second time before hitting the ground. All on board perished, including the first flight attendant to be killed while on duty, Alice Scribner, 26, of Chicago.[2]

---

[1] "Plane Crash Near Here Tuesday Night Kills 7," *Chesterton Tribune*, October 12, 1933.

[2] Ibid.

Investigators believed the plane was flying west on scheduled time and in apparently fine condition. Given the nature of the wreckage, the size of the debris field of the crash, and the testimony of dozens of witnesses, conclusions for the reason of the crash immediately focused on a bomb. Eventually, the U.S. Department of Commerce Aeronautics Branch concluded the aircraft was destroyed by an explosive device placed in the cargo hold, possibly a container of nitroglycerin attached to a timing device. Although no suspects were ever charged in the bombing, it was more likely a criminal attack than a politically motivated one.[3]

Attacks on aviation are like bad weather: they have always been present and always will be. Although there were numerous cases of violence perpetrated against passengers and aircraft from the 1930s onward, it wasn't until much later in the 20th century that security came to play a significant role in the overall development of the industry. There would be the occasional bombing at an airport or onboard an airliner somewhere in the world. And hijackings occurred more frequently as citizens of the Soviet-dominated East, and later Cuba, would take over flights to seek asylum in Western Europe or the United States. During this time, there were also numerous hijackings from the U.S. to Cuba. Most of the hijackers were running from the police; others were homesick or mentally unstable. They had no broader political agenda. As a result, safety was a far more important consideration to the industry's stakeholders. Security was on the industry's radar, but it was a distant, faint blip.

The Turning Point

The year 1968 was the turning point for the airline industry and its relationship with security. That year, for the first time in history, organized terrorists leveraged the air transport system to make a global, political statement. On July 23, members of the Popular Front for the Liberation of Palestine (PFPL) hijacked El Al flight 426, bound for Tel Aviv from Rome. The three hijackers ordered the Boeing 707 along with its 48 passengers and crew to Algiers. For some of the hostages, the ordeal lasted five weeks before their release, making it into one for the Guinness books as the longest hijacking on record. No one was killed and the plane was eventually returned to El Al.

Nevertheless, something far more important beyond the hijacking itself was taking place: the international media became fixated on the ordeal through-

[3] Andrew R. Thomas, *Aviation Insecurity: The New Challenges of Air Travel* (Amherst, NY: Prometheus Books, 2003), p. 140.

out its duration. Worldwide coverage on television, radio, and in newspapers was non-stop while the event played out. It seemed like a great soap opera was unfolding before the eyes of the world. For the PFPL, the wall-to-wall coverage of the hijacking was a boon to their cause. It provided them with more attention, publicity, and credibility than anything they could have possibly imagined.

The year before, in 1967, the Six-Day War between Israel and the Arab nations of Egypt, Iraq, Jordan, and Syria inexorably changed the landscape of the Middle East and the status of the Palestinian people. After the Suez Crisis of 1956, the United Nations set up peacekeepers along the Egypt-Israel border to separate both sides. In May 1967, Egyptian leader General Abdul Nasser said he would no longer honor the UN's mandate and began to amass troops along the border. Israel viewed this as an act of war and attacked on June 5. In addition to hitting Egypt, Israel also wiped out the air forces of its other perceived enemies on the first day. In less than a week, Israel's armies had advanced and captured Arab territory on the West Bank of the Jordan River, the Golan Heights, and the Sinai Desert. From a military point of view, it was a resounding success for Israel and a bitter defeat for the Arabs.

However, the victory also made Israel an occupier. The new lands she now controlled had more than 600,000 Palestinians already living there. With occupation, the seeds of the Palestinian-Israeli conflict, which were first sown at the end of World War II with the establishment of the state of Israel, were now blossoming into something even more complex than previously imagined. Palestinians had become prisoners in their own homes. It was natural that they would strike back and seek international attention to their plight.

Pablo Escobar—the Colombian cocaine kingpin who posed as Robin Hood and behaved like a butcher—got it right when he observed, "Terrorism is the atomic bomb of the world's poor and dispossessed." Undoubtedly, after the 1968 hijacking, a lot of people now hated the PFPL. But so what? The trade-off was that hundreds of millions of people had learned about their cause and were paying attention to what they had to say. Imagine what a multi-national corporation would have to spend to get that kind of global attention for its brands. As the famous Broadway producer George M. Cohan once said, "Any press is good press." This innovation—and let's admit that it was an innovation—spread as quickly as any new idea ever had. It was crystal clear now to any disgruntled, alienated, or oppressed group that disrupting anything airline-related would garner them a disproportionate amount of media attention.

In 1970, the PFPL followed up its earlier success with the "next generation" of airline attacks. Between September 6 and 13, the group hijacked four aircraft, carrying a total of 577 passengers and 39 crewmembers. Two of the airliners were flown to Dawson Field in Jordan, an old World War II facility built by the British. Another plane was flown to Beirut, and the fourth to Cairo. After several days of negotiations that resulted in some of their comrades being released from foreign prisons, all of the passengers and crew were let go unharmed. Then, the two airliners in Jordan and the one in Cairo were blown up and completely destroyed. Again, international media coverage was wall-to-wall, complete for the first time with talking heads offering expert analysis and opinion.[4] This was also the beginning of many of the security measures we experience today: passenger screening machines, passenger profiling, and armed police at airports were all introduced. The international community began rapidly passing conventions requiring specific procedures and began training for compliance to those procedures.

In 1985, members of Hezbollah hijacked TWA flight 847 en route from Athens to Rome. NBC dedicated two-thirds of its entire news coverage to the story during the three-week ordeal. Further, the *New York Times, Washington Post*, and *Los Angeles Times* ran a combined 629 stories on it.[5] The bombing of Pan Am Flight 108 over Lockerbie, Scotland was given "saturation coverage" as well.[6] Few who were alive will forget the wrenching video of Susan Cohen crying, "Not my baby," as she collapsed in front of a group of reporters at JFK Airport. While no group initially took credit, the international coverage of several Middle Eastern conflicts received dramatic spikes.[7]

As this innovation continued to gain traction, the global air transport system was now *the* prime venue, as political and religious groups—and their terrorist colleagues—played a deadly game of cat and mouse, the objective of which was global attention and publicity and, later, mass casualties and catastrophic destruction. This was enhanced by the ease with which it was possible to sabotage an aircraft or an airport. Blowing up an aircraft really only requires one person to build a device and the same or another person to

---

[4] The most comprehensive chronology of attacks against civil aviation ever put together is by Mary F. Schiavo. It was published in Volume I of *Aviation Security Management* (Westport, CT: Praeger Security International, 2008) pp. 142-260.

[5] Brigette Nacos, et. al., "Terrorism and the Print Media: The 1985 TWA Hostage Crisis," *Terrorism an International Journal 12*, p. 109.

[6] John Harrison, "Supply Chain Security and International Terrorism" in Volume of 1 of *Supply Chain Security* ed. by Andrew R. Thomas (Westport, CT: Praeger Security International, 2009), p. 57.

[7] Ibid.

set it off. For all of the over-analysis of 9/11, let's not forget that only 19 men actually executed the plan—and it's still unclear whether all of the terrorists knew they were going to die that day.

In the following years, groups including the Croatian Ustaja Movement, Basque ETA, Irish Republican Army, Colombia's FARC, Sri Lanka's Tamil Tigers, and Al-Qaeda would look to demonstrate their reach, grab headlines, and exact revenge by destroying airplanes, airports, and killing innocents. It continues unabated today.

The Scourge of Our Time

Since 9/11, governments around the world have spent obscene sums of money, time, and other resources—and hassled billions of innocent people—in order to prevent the next big terrorist attack. Politicians on both side of the aisle have resolutely said that America is in a decades-long war against terrorists who seek to destroy our way of life and kill us in large numbers. Although the Republicans under George W. Bush first espoused this view while the fires were still burning hot at the World Trade Center and Pentagon, the Democrats under Barack Obama have been no less verbose in their chest-beating, all to "protect America" and "secure the homeland."

If I sound a bit cynical that the government of the U.S. has overstated the nature of the terror threat, it is only because I am deeply distrustful of what our government has done—or not done—since 9/11. In the realm of airport security, for example, why do we pat down 6-year old children and World War II Medal of Honor recipients, while not properly checking the background of the hundreds of thousands of people who work at our nation's airports, people who have unlimited access to planes, cargo, and baggage? Or, if there are so many terrorists out there wanting to kills us, why we have done next to nothing to keep millions of people from simply walking into the U.S. from Mexico or Canada, as they have since 9/11? It makes one wonder if the threat is something other than we are being told.

But before I go on, I admit that I believe Al-Qaeda, even after the death of Osama Bin Laden, is "in it for the long run." Islamic terrorists and other terrorist groups, some who have not even been created yet, will continue to try to destroy commercial aviation assets. And, despite what we do or don't do, aviation will be front and center in their planning. Unless we kill every one of them, which is not possible, aviation will always be threatened—and attacked.

As evidence of this long view, there has been a lot of speculation as to why Al-Qaeda decided to launch its greatest attack on September 11, 2001. Was it merely a coincidence? Or was there a significance of the day to Osama Bin Laden and his cohorts?

The most plausible explanation is rooted in Al-Qaeda's mysticism. If you read the writings of Al-Qaeda's leaders—living and dead—it becomes clear very quickly that they believe in the interconnectedness of history over centuries. Their writings can be quite interesting. Like many extremists, Al-Qaeda's leaders have thought of themselves more as intellectuals than anything else. In the same vein as Lenin's Soviets, Hitler's Nazis, Mao's Communists, and Pol Pot's Khmer Rouge, the leaders write a lot. A simple Google search will reveal the volumes that Al-Qaeda's founders and leaders have published for public consumption.

Underpinning much of the narrative is the notion that the Muslim world has been subjugated to the West for centuries and needs to strike back now, before the West conquers Islam. This gives justification to whatever Al-Qaeda does because it is done defensively: to protect the vestiges of traditional Islam from ever-expanding foreign aggression. This is a powerful message. It is right and just to blow yourself up and kill innocents; you will be guaranteed eternal life in paradise because you are defending all that is sacred from the imperialists. This is nothing new in human history, nor is it unique to only Islam. The Christian millenialists and mass movements of the 12th and 13th centuries massacred hundreds of thousands, maybe millions, of "non-believers" across Europe to "defend the faith." Hindu extremists were the first ones to deploy female suicide bombers.

For Al-Qaeda, in the context of centuries, the date of September 11, 1683, is important. This was a seminal event in human history, especially for the followers of Islam. This was the day when the decline of Muslim power got fully underway. Although the defeat of the Moors by Spain in the 15th century was a big blow to Islamic ambitions, the defeat at the Battle of Vienna in 1683 was something the Muslim world has never really recovered from.

That summer, a Turkish Army of 100,000 strong marched quickly and easily across Eastern Europe, defeating every opponent along the way and arriving at the gates of Vienna in July. It laid siege to the city and waited. A 4th grader looking at a map of Europe could easily discern that if Vienna were to fall, the rest of the Danube's cities, and eventually Western Europe, would go as well. As the summer wore on, it seemed inevitable that Vienna would succumb and the Ottoman Empire might conceivably control all of Christendom.

But history has a way of shredding inevitability. During the night of September 11, a Polish army, marching under the cross, attacked the sleeping Turks and pushed them back from Vienna. Although the Ottoman Empire lasted until the early 20th century, it was most often on the defensive against Europeans and others from that day forward. September 11, 1683 was the high tide of the Ottomans, as the Battle of Gettysburg was for the Confederacy. They never got that far north again. As Winston Churchill might have said, the defeat at Vienna was "the beginning of the beginning of the end" for Ottoman power.

So Al-Qaeda believes in the interconnectivity of history. This means that today there are a group of people, probably numbering in the thousands around the world, who believe that God is on their side and that blowing up our airplanes and airports is the best way to wage war against their enemies. They will keep trying. But given the size and scope of the global air transport system, even spectacular attacks like 9/11 should not bring things to a halt, unless we *allow* it to happen.

Here is a key point: in response to this incredibly small group of highly motivated individuals whose only real power comes from what we give them, Americans (and many others across the world) have inexorably altered their way of life and allowed their governments to fight questionable wars and intrude on their rights, all in exchange for a façade of security against a group of guys who live on the run and under constant threat of capture or death.

What We Do to Ourselves

The lesson should be clear: what the terrorists do to us is not nearly as painful as what we do to ourselves after they attack. And this is exactly what the terrorists have in mind: to cause relatively small damage that cascades into far bigger costs and expenditures. This is not to say that there wasn't terrible individual death and suffering because of 9/11. There was. Nearly 3,000 innocent people were slaughtered. It also doesn't mean that there won't be other big attacks where thousands, maybe even tens of thousands, of innocent people are murdered. It is likely to occur. Still, the U.S. is a nation of 315 million people. Our existence as a nation will never be in jeopardy because of what terrorists do.

The misguided hope in the aftermath of the 9/11 attacks was that by eliminating the conflicts that had plagued the FAA for decades, and creating the TSA, aviation security would finally be professionalized in America—once and for all. However, despite all of the good intentions and $75 billion spent to date, this has not been the case. The TSA has been a major disappointment. Dishearteningly, even John Mica, the Republican Congressman from Florida who was the person on Capitol Hill most responsible for creating

TSA in the first place, now describes the TSA as "my bastard child and a monster that we've created, a bureaucratic monster."[8]

In fact, the more TSA has done to "protect" us, the more it has actually led to greater numbers of our deaths, by compelling more folks to opt-out of flying and take far more dangerous car trips. Newer security measures like the enhanced pat-down procedures and the intrusive naked X-ray machines have passengers wondering: should I accept all the humiliation and hassle with security that comes with flying to my destination? Or should I drive to my destination? Recent surveys about the hassle factor caused by the aviation security process reveal the tipping point for many Americans about whether to fly or drive is now six hours.[9] But here's the rub: driving is logarithmically more dangerous than taking a plane. Since September 2001, about 350,000 Americans have been killed on our nation's roads.[10] Conversely, less than a dozen individuals have been killed in terrorist-related attacks against our national aviation system, and the number of air passengers lost in mechanical or weather-related accidents is in the hundreds. In short, the less people fly and the more they drive, the larger the death toll.

This again reveals that the greatest damage inflicted in the age of terrorism comes most often from what we do to ourselves. While Al-Qaeda and its cohorts are highly motivated, they simply don't pose an existential threat to our way of life. The reason they used our cargo aircraft to attempt to deliver toner cartridge bombs in October 2010 is because they don't possess the platforms to deliver destruction on their own. The longer-lasting impact from an attack comes within. Whether it is spending billions of dollars to take away nail clippers, touching our "junk" (which had its 15 minutes of fame when a young passenger reacted to an intrusion by a TSA screener who was getting too close to his private parts), or forcing more people onto the roads, our reactions are what cause the most ache.

The "Booty Bomb" and A Day in Our Future

In our future lies a day in which multiple suicide passengers on multiple planes blow themselves up through the detonation of body-cavity bombs hidden within them. Al Qaeda has developed the tactic that allows suicide

---

[8] Interview with John Mica (R-Florida) in the documentary *Please Remove Your Shoes* produced and directed by Fred Grevalt.

[9] Gary Stoller, "Poll: Most Fliers Angered or Bothered by TSA Pat-Downs," *USA Today*, November 23, 2010, www.usatoday.com/travel/flights/2010-11-23-airport-security-tsa-poll_N.htm.

[10] This comes from the Fatality Accident Reporting System (FARS), which is put out by the National Highway Traffic Safety Agency (www-fars.nhtsa.dot.gov/Main/index.aspx).

bombers to breach even the tightest security. Based upon methods used in the illegal drug trade for years, Al-Qaeda has developed a way for the human body cavity to become the delivery system for concealed explosives.

In August 2009, inside a palace in Saudi Arabia, the scene was the bloody aftermath of an Al-Qaeda attack aimed at killing Prince Mohammed Bin Nayef, head of Saudi Arabia's counter terrorism operations. To get his bomb into this room, Abdullah Asieri, one of Saudi Arabia's most wanted men, avoided detection by two sets of airport security, including metal detectors and palace security guards who patted him down thoroughly. He then spent 30 hours in the close company of the prince's own secret service agents—all without anyone suspecting a thing.[11]

Asieri had a pound of high explosives plus a detonator inserted in his rectum. This was a meticulously planned operation with Al-Qaeda once again producing something new: this time, the Trojan bomber. The blast left the prince lightly wounded—a failure as an assassination, but as an exercise in defeating security, it was perfect.

To get so close, the bomber persuaded the prince he wanted to leave Al-Qaeda and had some important intelligence information to share. On the Internet, Al-Qaeda has an animated movie showing the meeting between the bomber and the prince. Asieri says more senior Al-Qaeda figures want to surrender and convinces the prince to talk to them on a cell phone.

In the conversation recorded by al Qaeda, you hear a beep in the middle of two identical phrases that are repeated by the bomber and his handler. The beep was likely a text message that activated the bomb concealed inside Asieri. The Trojan bomber hands the phone to Prince Mohammed. He's standing next to him, and 14 seconds later, he detonates.

Having already tested and deployed the body cavity bomb, it will be only be a matter of time before Al-Qaeda or others uses this "innovation" against commercial airplanes. All of the current and future security measures at our nation's airports—even the naked x-ray machines—won't be able to locate a body-cavity bomb. Not to reveal too much here, but we should be aware that there are smart, evil people out there doing little more than trying to figure out new ways how to inflict harm and pain on other human beings.

---

[11] To see the compelling video, visit CBS' coverage of the attack at www.cbsnews.com/stories/2009/09/28/eveningnews/main5347847.shtml.

Changing the Current Course

The current aviation security strategy of always doing more and subjecting passengers to worse is not sustainable. The logical conclusion to the current path is to make millions of annual air travelers strip and undergo a body cavity search or spend billions and billions to develop technology that will be similarly intrusive but in a different way. Imagine that. But before we get to this Kafkaesque outcome, we have the opportunity to change course—to implement the kind of aviation security system that is truly malleable, dynamic, risk-based, and efficient, to use the TSA's own words. The alternative in the form of the status quo is increasingly unacceptable—and dangerous.

Much of the international community has been critical of TSA's "more and more" approach to security on a regular basis. One of the more outspoken critics is Sir Martin Broughton, the chairman of British Airways. In an April 2011 speech before the Chartered Institute of Logistics and Transport in London, Mr. Broughton criticized the TSA for its one-size-fits-all approach. He asked, "Is it sensible to run exactly the same security checks on pilots—each and every time they fly—as, for example, a Yemeni student?" Some would describe this as profiling, "which some people regard as a pejorative term" with "discriminatory overtones," but such concerns were misplaced. "Making everybody suffer inconvenience in the name of uniformity doesn't make any sense at all and reduces the quality of security by dissipating resources."[12]

Change is not easy. There are 10 years of institutionalized dysfunction at the TSA to overcome. To build on what Sir Martin says, the best place to start might be to re-allocate our scarce resources in ways that make a measurable contribution to making the airline travel experience better and safer. This begins by revisiting and finally living up to some fundamental principles of successful security practice. They are derived from my study of extensive aviation security since the late 1990s.

Security Principle #1: Technology and the latest machines are not the most important elements. People come first; ideas are second; expensive gadgets and gizmos are a distant third.

Since 9/11, despite the deployment of expensive database programs and things like puffers and naked x-ray machines, there have only been really

---

[12] A transcript of the entire speech can be found at the *Financial Times'* web site at www.ft.com/cms/s/0/bd6dab94-6acf-11e0-9744-00144feab49a.html#ixzz1K4CQBqJC.

two substantive improvements to aviation security: first and foremost is the pro-active involvement of passengers in the security process and second is the re-enforced cockpit door. Neither one of these has anything to do with all of the stuff that has been tested, bought, and deployed by the TSA.

Prior to 9/11, passengers and flight crew were expected to "take it sitting down" when an incident occurred in the air. Now, they've become front-line troops. All of the major attacks against U.S. airliners that have been thwarted since 9/11 were stopped because of human action: the shoe bomber was stopped and subdued by a flight attendant and other passengers; the underwear bomber was taken down by his seatmates; the liquid explosive bombers were given up to British authorities by their neighbors and friends. In a great irony, the willingness of passengers to get involved and provide this most critical measure of security had nothing to do with TSA and the billions it has spent. Instead, it is the terrorists' own actions on 9/11 that compelled everyone onboard a flight to get involved in securing the aircraft.

Also, as mentioned in Chapter 6, the cockpit door was the major security flaw that the 9/11 terrorists exploited. Now that it's always closed and much sturdier, the likelihood of a hijacking is almost nil.

> *Security Principle #2: Professionalization is the best path to a competent security organization.*

Those who work in aviation security possess fewer certifications and formal credentials than barbers do, and this is not to insult barbers. The point is that anyone with the basic skill set of a high school graduate can become a screener or a manager for TSA. Ten years after 9/11, there are less than a dozen academic programs where someone can actually study transportation security management.

Security is often confused with law enforcement, and many of TSA's early managers came from organizations like the FBI and police departments. The job of doing security is a specialized endeavor that requires a unique perspective, different than law enforcement. Police officers are inherently reactive in nature. Their primary responsibility is to catch people who break the law. While there is a proactive element in law enforcement—think street cops walking the beat—most of what they do is geared towards responding to something that has already happened.

People who do security for a living need to be much more proactive, especially when it comes to dealing with suicidal terrorists. In the past 15 years, almost every major terrorist attack against commercial aviation was perpetrated by an individual or individuals willing to die for the mission. On 9/11, once the terrorists gained access to the aircraft, there was nothing that could be done, short of what the passengers and flight crew on United Flight 93 did when they fought back.

The number of schools where an aviation security management curriculum is available is even smaller. Such a lack of educational opportunities means that unless something is done quickly, the tens of thousands of new aviation security managers who will join the profession in the coming years will not have had the opportunity to learn the best in transportation security research and practice. To professionalize the field of aviation security management, several requirements need to be met. First and foremost, there must be a body of knowledge and a repertoire of behaviors and skills needed in the practice of the profession—knowledge, behavior, and skills that are not normally possessed by the non-professional. To date, very little of that body of knowledge and repertoire exists in a clear and cogent format.

As evidence of this lack of professionalization is the fact that the TSA folks who work at the nation's airport checkpoints are not law-enforcement officers. Despite their nice uniforms and shiny badges, TSA screeners have none of the power a policeman has. They can't arrest or detain a passenger. This is why at every checkpoint in America you see local police officers stationed. They are the ones who can enforce the law, not the TSA workers. Failing to professionalize the TSA's 40,000-plus screeners has resulted in huge turnover, low morale, and poor performance within the organization.

Security Principle #3: Intelligence data is the best weapon.

The most powerful weapon against terrorists before they get to the airport or on-board an aircraft is carefully collected intelligence data. Physical security measures are of limited use when it comes to battling the bad guys. Unfortunately, the history of aviation security has tended to favor measures over intelligence in every sense of the word. Even more upsetting, these measures are usually used to fight the most recent battle and designed to stop an attack that has already occurred: think of taking off your shoes, discarding your liquids prior to entering the checkpoint, and being subjected to a pat-down or naked x-ray screening. All of these are reactions to prior attacks. As the terrorists evolve, the current system retards. Intelligence is essential to reducing—not eliminating—the persistent threat to the airline industry. It gives us the ability to stay at least one step ahead, rather than three steps behind.

Security Principle #4: The focus needs to be on bad people instead of bad things.

Since its creation, the TSA has overwhelmingly focused on keeping bad things out of airports and off aircraft. This has been and will always be the wrong approach. Aviation is a human endeavor. The threats come to the system from human beings. The vulnerabilities are human creations. An airport is a city with three neighborhoods: the landside, the terminal, and the ramp. To do the best job possible to protect the system, we must know the residents of each of those areas as well as who is visiting the city. We must look more at keeping bad people away from airports and aircraft than anything else.

Security Principle #5: Profiling is to some degree necessary.

The need to look at certain passengers differently than others from a security perspective only makes sense. To try to argue against this point is silly. Therefore, measures should be in place that profile those passengers and visitors who provide a higher level of threat. Moreover, as threats evolve and change, profiles must change, too.

For the airline industry, security is one of those "known unknowns" going forward. Aviation will remain in the cross hairs of international terrorists. We know attempts will be made to kill people and hurt the system. We also are pretty sure who will try. What we don't know is when and how. By continuing on the current trajectory of reacting to what the terrorists do in order to shape our strategy, we will always be needlessly wasting scarce resources and unnecessarily hassling passengers.

The Future

Travel is fatal to prejudice, bigotry, and narrow-mindedness, and many of our people need it sorely on these accounts. Broad, wholesome, charitable views of men and things cannot be acquired by vegetating in one little corner of the earth all one's lifetime.

—From Mark Twain's *Innocents Abroad*

Turbulence Ahead for Airline Unions and High-Paying Jobs

"Deregulation will be the greatest thing to happen to the airlines since the jet engine."

—Richard Ferris, former CEO United Airlines, 1976

Since the advent of air travel, airlines have regularly fallen apart and been put back together by government and the courts. Whether through mergers and acquisitions or bankruptcies, the industry regularly reconfigures and reinvents itself. Here are some of the more noteworthy bankruptcies in the U.S. in recent years: Frontier (2008); ATA (2008); Delta (2005); Northwest (2005); US Airways for the second time (2004); United (2002); US Airways (2002); TWA for the third and last time (2001); Pan Am for the second and last time (1998); TWA (1995); TWA (1992); Eastern (1991); Continental (1991); Pan Am (1991). On the merger side of things, some recent ones include Southwest/Air Tran (2011), United/Continental (2010), Delta/Northwest (2008), US Airways/America West (2005), and Air Tran/ValuJet 1997.[1]

Caught in the midst of all of this tumult are the people who do the work every day to keep the planes flying safe and sound. They are a tough bunch and face uncertainty about their future employment all the time. In 1948, the airline industry saw its largest merger to date when Pan Am acquired American Overseas Airlines (A.O.A.). When asked about the future of the A.O.A. employees, a spokesman for Pan Am said, "We will take over the workers of American Overseas Airlines and try to find suitable employment for them within the Pan-American organization."[2] Within two years, thousands of former A.O.A. employees were out on the street. As you saw in Chapter 6, tens of thousands of airline employees lost their jobs in the wake of the 9/11 attacks. A career in the airline industry is clearly not for the faint of heart.[3]

For those who have been able to keep their jobs, they are likely less well-off today than in the past. Chesley "Sully" Sullenberger is the pilot who heroically landed US Airways Flight 1549 on the Hudson River after it was struck by a flock of birds. In testimony before the House Transportation and Infrastructure Committee, Sullenberger and his co-pilot, Jeffrey Skiles, detailed how their salaries have fallen exponentially in recent years as US Airways went through two bankruptcy reorganizations.

"The bankruptcies were used by some as a fishing expedition to get what they could not get in normal times," Sullenberger said of the airlines. He said the problems began with the deregulation of the industry in the 1970s, which was promised to be a panacea for the airlines and their employees

---

[1] Compiled from various media and industry reports.

[2] Associated Press, "Two Airlines Consolidate," *St. Petersburg Times*, December 13, 1948, p. 3.

[3] In full disclosure, my home is a union home. I am a member of the AAUP (American Association of University Professors), and my wife carries a Cleveland Teachers Union card in her wallet. For a while, I was also a member of the Writers Guild. We are not always in agreement with what our unions do in our name. Moreover, given the nature of our current locals, we cannot opt out. Still, at the end, we have benefitted from being members of unions.

moving forward. The reduced compensation has placed "pilots and their families in an untenable financial situation," Sullenberger said. "I do not know a single professional airline pilot who wants his or her children to follow in their footsteps."[4]

Skiles said unless federal laws are revised to improve labor-management relations, "experienced crews in the cockpit will be a thing of the past." And Sullenberger added that without experienced pilots, "we will see negative consequences to the flying public."

Sullenberger himself has started a consulting business to help make ends meet. Skiles added, "For the last six years, I have worked seven days a week between my two jobs just to maintain a middle class standard of living."[5]

In 2004, while Sullenberger's employer US Airways was reorganizing for the second time under Chapter 11 bankruptcy protection, the judge overseeing the airline's filing ordered a 21 percent pay cut for the majority of its 28,000 employees. The airline, which had asked for a 23 percent cut, was still pleased when Judge Steven S. Mitchell said he "reluctantly" agreed with US Airways that without the cost savings it could be forced out of business. "This is a ticking fiscal time bomb," Mitchell said of the airline's precarious financial position. Although his action "will result in financial hardship for the employees," Mitchell said the alternative of liquidation would force employees to find jobs possibly at even lower wages in a shrinking airline industry.[6] US Airways chief executive Bruce R. Lakefield called the cuts a "regrettable but necessary step" in the airline's reorganization. "Our mission is to save as many jobs as possible."[7] During its earlier Chapter 11 reorganization in 2002, US Airways employees agreed to 5 to 15 percent in pay cuts.

In the past decade, every major U.S. airline has engaged in some type of restructuring in an attempt to avoid the termination of its business. One of the airlines' most effective means for doing so is acquiring cost-cutting concessions from their labor forces. Ten years ago, salaries and benefits accounted for nearly 40 percent of industry expenses. Now they account for less than 30 percent.

---

[4] "Chesley "Sully" Sullenberger To Congress: My Pay Has Been Cut 40 Percent In Recent Years, Pension Terminated," *Huffington Post*, February 24, 2009, www.huffingtonpost.com/2009/02/24/chesley-sully-sullenberge_0_n_169512.html.

[5] Ibid.

[6] Keith Alexander, "Judge Allows Airline Pay Cuts: US Airways Workers Begin Quiet Protest," *Washington Post*, October 16, 2004, p. E1.

[7] Ibid.

The Empty Seat Syndrome

While the reduction in the number of airline employees, along with their wages and benefits, is part of the industry's broader Flying Cheap strategy, there are also structural reasons why the employee side of the industry has always been unstable. The Empty Seat Syndrome is one of the biggest. As with many businesses, the products the airlines sell are fixed and perishable. That is, they exist for a particular moment in time and then go away forever. The offering of a seat on next Monday's 2:45 p.m. flight to Newark is set months in advance and the airline does all that it can to fill it. It knows full well that once the doors on that plane close, the ability to sell the seat evaporates into oblivion. The same is true for tickets to a baseball game, the table at your local restaurant, and hotel rooms. For companies in this kind of business, it becomes critical to manage the capacity of their facilities the right way. Historically, the airlines haven't been able to do it very well.

To be fair, getting the capacity right for the airlines is incredibly difficult even in the best of conditions. The complexity and variability inherent to the industry, along with the knowledge that government will be there to step in if things get really bad, make it nearly impossible to effectively deal with the capacity challenge. Consequently, the airlines are in a constant crisis mode when it comes to deciding which planes to fly; how many routes to add or end; and, ultimately, how many employees they will need—or not need—to make it all happen.

The pattern goes like this: when times are good, the airlines buy airplanes and add capacity like it's going out of style. Inevitably, the economy turns down, fuel prices rise, or a Black Swan event occurs and things fall apart. The most recent economic downturn in 2008 still has much of America—and the world—reeling from the fallout. In the United States, the airlines quickly recognized a need to reduce capacity within the system. The problem they face—and one that has always been a source of great stress—is trying to figure out where the route shifts need to happen. They hope to do this before they lose too much money serving areas that are going in the wrong direction. In the last five years, for example, air service most often dropped at midsize airports and cities where jobs disappeared or housing prices collapsed. Las Vegas, Phoenix, and Detroit all lost flights in the 12 months that ended in March 2011. But traffic has risen at airports where the regional economies have fared better, including Denver, San Francisco, and Charlotte.[8]

---

[8] Jad Mouawad, "Air Service Cutbacks Hit Hardest Where Recession Did," *New York Times*, July 8, 2011, www.nytimes.com/2011/07/09/business/flight-cutbacks-hit-midsize-airports-hardest.html?pagewanted=print.

This difficulty in forecasting is exacerbated when industry leaders make decisions that have no real basis in reality. In the summer of 2011, with economic uncertainty and high-fuel prices firmly in place, American Airlines announced the biggest aircraft order in history. The carrier will acquire 20 Boeing 737 Next Generation aircraft per year from 2013 to 2017. The planes could be 737-700, 737-800, or 737-900 ER aircraft. American said it also expects to receive 100 Boeing 737 Next Generation "re-engine" aircraft, which will be equipped with new and more fuel-efficient engines. Subject to Boeing approval of the re-engined aircraft program, American said it would receive 20 of the planes per year from 2018 to 2022. Further, American said it will lease 130 Airbus current generation A320 family aircraft, which could be A319, A320, or A321 planes. They expect 20 to 35 of the planes to be delivered each year from 2013 to 2017. American also committed to purchase 130 Airbus A320 family "new-engine option" aircraft, which will have new, more fuel-efficient engines. Ten of the new-engine aircraft are scheduled to be delivered in 2017, followed by 20 to 25 each year from 2018 to 2022.[9]

Here's the rub: American Airlines hasn't turned a profit since 2007. Undaunted by this little fact, the two major aircraft manufacturers nevertheless agreed to fully finance the first 230 planes, for somewhere around $13 billion, leasing them back to American so the carrier won't have to further harm its already weak balance sheet.[10] American CEO Gerard Arpey defended the deal, saying, "We have a long track record of meeting our obligations to all of our stakeholders." He was alluding to the fact that American is one of the few network carriers not to have flown through bankruptcy in the past decade. Nevertheless, it remains stuck with high labor costs and a heavy debt burden, not to mention a hard rivalry with Southwest Airlines in its Texas base.[11] So, while the other major carriers considered an acceleration of their cuts in capacity by the end of 2011 once the busy summer travel period ended, American placed the biggest aircraft order in aviation history. In the five months through May 2011, 295 of 500 airports in the nation had fewer flights than in the same period last year. In 2010, 315 airports reported fewer flights than the previous year, compared with 414 in

---

[9] Matt Joyce, "American details delivery schedule for new planes," *Dallas Business Journal*, July 25, 2011, www.bizjournals.com/dallas/news/2011/07/25/American-details-delivery.html.

[10] Holman W. Jenkins, Jr., "Plane Crazy: How American Airlines won the lottery," *Wall Street Journal*, July 25, 2011, http://online.wsj.com/article/SB10001424053111903554904576461870056566168.html?KEYWORDS=plane+crazy.

[11] Ibid.

2009. Nearly 200 airports, most of them tiny and many in remote places, have lost air service entirely since 2008.[12]

In Indianapolis, for example, airline mergers, sky-high fuel prices, and the global recession have grounded about 13.5 percent of the daily scheduled flights from Indianapolis International Airport over the past five years and severed direct connections to several cities. Nonstop flights from Indianapolis to Austin, San Antonio, Hartford, and San Francisco have been halted. And the number of daily round trips to New York's LaGuardia has been reduced. An average of 153 flights depart each day from the airport on non-stop trips to 35 other cities. In 2006, an average of 177 flights took off daily to 40 cities.[13] Northwest was once the most active carrier in Indianapolis, with 42 daily flights in 2006, before it merged with Delta. Separately, the two airlines had 58 daily flights. Now, the merged operation averages about 40 flights a day.[14] Given this roller-coaster ride of low and high capacity, it is little wonder why employees always seem to be on the short end of the stick.

Unions and the Airline Industry in the U.S.

Since 1936, labor/management relations in the airline industry have been overseen by the Railway Labor Act (45 U.S.C. §§151-188). The act previously applied only to the nation's railroad industry under the original 1926 legislation. It was amended ten years later to include the employees of the burgeoning airline industry. The idea behind the RLA is pretty simple: in order to avoid disruptions to America's transport network through strikes and other kinds of work stoppages, the act imposed mandatory mediation and gave the President the ability to order workers back to work. In exchange for this Presidential authority, the RLA gave workers the guaranteed right to organize for the purpose of negotiating a collective bargaining agreement.

The airline industry has been a bellwether for the labor movement as a whole in the United States since President Reagan fired striking air traffic controllers in 1981. Today, around 80 percent of airline workers are unionized. This makes the airlines some of the most heavily unionized companies in America. The airline unions are constituted along the lines of what they do: there are separate unions for pilots, flight attendants, baggage handlers,

---

[12] Ibid.

[13] Bruce C. Smith, "Fewer Flights are taking off from Indy," *Indianapolis Star*, July 20, 2011, www.indystar.com/article/20110720/BUSINESS/107200323/Fewer-flights-taking-off-from-Indy.

[14] Ibid.

mechanics, customer service agents, and flight instructors. The Airline Pilots Association (ALPA) is the largest pilots' union, while the Association of Flight Attendants (AFA) represents most flight attendants. Most mechanics and baggage handlers belong to the International Association of Machinists (IAM).

Because the airlines are out spread across the entire nation and the world, the RLA mandates that a bargaining unit must include all of the workers of the same job classification throughout an entire company. By requiring unions to organize on a companywide basis, the RLA helps to avoid the creation of a patchwork of work rules that piecemeal unionization at specific facilities would bring. This standardization ensures that airlines will function in a much smoother, more efficient manner.

Though the industry is highly unionized, the unions are extremely fragmented. For example, three different unions represent flight attendants (including the AFA, the Transport Workers Union at Southwest, and the Independent Association of Professional Flight Attendants at American). Moreover, while unions representing different work groups have formed coalitions across airlines, the craft structure of the unions and the dramatic pay disparities between different work groups represent barriers to building solidarity. Without solidarity, the individual unions are at a disadvantage when trying to get their way with the carriers.

Pilots represent the elite of the airline workforce, with some pilots at the big carriers still making up to $200,000 a year. Yet junior pilots at the outsourced regional jet carriers can make as little as $15,000 a year. This big pay difference between the large carriers and the regionals, which make up 50 percent of all air traffic, applies to flight attendants as well. Even within the same bargaining units, mechanics get higher pay than other ground workers. Customer service agents, meanwhile, are among the lowest paid of all airline workers. There is strength in numbers, so long as those numbers share a common interest. When it comes to the airline unions, however, unity is much easier said than accomplished.

Eating Their Own

The history of the labor movement in the United States has been marked by struggles with management and companies, and also among the workers and unions themselves. The weaknesses driven by the inherent divisions between the airline unions are made worse by infighting that stems from mergers and acquisitions. The 2008 merger of Delta and Northwest Airlines, which created the world's largest airline at the time, is a strong case study about the difficulties employees face as they deal with the upheaval that characterizes the industry. The blending of Delta's largely non-union workers and Northwest's union workforce was going be a challenge for sure, but no one could predict just how just hard it would be for the unions. More than 50,000 employees ultimately voted on whether to unionize—the single largest private-sector vote to unionize since the United Auto Workers organized the Ford Motor Company in 1941.[15]

Employees voted against unionization in five different elections. On March 1, 2010, Delta's simulator technicians voted on whether to join the International Association of Machinists and Aerospace Workers. IAM lost after receiving only 40 votes out of 91 in the bargaining unit.[16] On November 4, 2010, 94 percent of an eligible 19,877 flight attendants rejected unionization by the AFA.[17]

On November 19, 2010, fleet service employees turned down the IAM, with 5,571 of the 13,104 eligible voters voting against unionization. The IAM received 4,909 votes, with the rest of the employees in the bargaining unit abstaining.[18] On November 23, 2010, 439 out of 673 stock and stores (maintenance department plane parts inventory control) employees voted against joining IAM.[19] On December 8, 2010, 8,746 out of an eligible 15,436 passenger service employees cast "no" votes against union representation.[20]

These results shouldn't be too surprising, as most airline employees aren't your typical card-carrying union members. Membership meetings at airline unions occur infrequently—the constant travel inherent for pilots and flight attendants certainly contributes to this problem—and rank-and-file participation is generally reserved for contract-negotiation times. Most members generally regard their unions as service providers for negotiations and

---

[15] Mike Esterl, "Barbs Fly in Union Fight," *Wall Street Journal*, October 21, 2010, http://online.wsj.com/article/SB10001424052702303339504575566490276252822.html?KEYWORDS=barbs+fly+i n+union+fight.

[16] Delta Air Lines, Inc., 37 N.M.B. No. 29 (2010), www.nmb.gov/representation/deter2010/37n029.pdf

[17] Taylor Leake, "Delta Flight Attendants Union Grounded... for Now," *Change.org*, November 5, 2010, http://news.change.org/stories/delta-flight-attendants-union-grounded-for-now.

[18] Delta Air Lines, Inc., Fleet Service Employees, 38 N.M.B. No. 14 (2010), www.nmb.gov/representation/deter2011/38n014.pdf.

[19] Delta Air Lines, Inc., Stock and Stores Employees, 38 N.M.B. No. 15 (2010), www.nmb.gov/representation/deter2011/38n015.pdf.

[20] Delta Air Lines, Inc., Passenger Service Employees, 38 N.M.B. No. 16 (2010), www.nmb.gov/representation/deter2011/38n016.pdf.

grievances. Many assume that this is what they pay dues for and expect the union to function, in the words of one veteran activist, as "a giant grievance machine."[21]

As new mergers unfold, they often pit two competing unions against each for the members, and their dues, of the new entity. The case of which future union would represent all of the 25,000 flight attendants at the new United/Continental illustrates how ugly this can get. A dispute arose where different unions (the IAM at Continental and the AFA at United) represented the flight attendants at each airline. As the merger has resulted in a single carrier, the IAM union (which represented roughly 9,500 flight attendants at Continental and Continental Micronesia) was forced to defend its turf against the numerically larger AFA (15,000 flight attendants at United). Unsurprisingly, the Machinists lost. The Machinists (IAM), however, cried foul, claiming the AFA engaged in what amounts to so-called union busting.[22]

According to an IAM statement: "The IAM is protesting the conduct of the recent representation election for Flight Attendants at United Airlines, Continental Airlines, and Continental Micronesia." The victorious AFA responded by saying, "Throughout the entire campaign the tactics employed by the IAM were some of the nastiest we've ever seen in other organizing drives where we faced management and union busters of the worst kind. Flight Attendants saw through it, voted for AFA, and now they want to move on with a unified Flight Attendant group."[23] As unions battle with each other for supremacy, they don't have the resources to wage the struggle for greater salaries and benefits. This keeps the airlines, even with all of their own challenges, in a stronger position.

The View in Europe

Across the 27-nation European Union, somewhere around 330 airlines provide regularly scheduled air transport. Approximately 500 airports handle traffic of the EU's nearly 500 million annual passengers, of which 25 handle upwards of at least 10 million passengers a year. In scope and scale, the EU airline system is similar to America's.

Most airline employees in Europe, as in America, are members of unions. A big difference between the two, though, is the nature of the airlines

---

[21] Jenalia Moreno, "Labor Issues Key to Airline Merger Success," *Houston Chronicle*, April 30, 2010, www.chron.com/disp/story.mpl/business/6984637.html#ixzz1T1iu5MNd.

[22] Ibid.

[23] Ibid.

themselves. Whereas shareholders have privately held carriers in the U.S. for decades, most of Europe's big airlines were state-owned until quite recently. British Airways went private in 1987; Lufthansa in 1994; Air France partially so in 1997; Alitalia in 2008. As the air system in Europe developed quickly after World War II, the emergence of state-owned airlines was paralleled by the rising power of their unionized employees, who were by definition government employees. Working with management, which was also part of the governmental structure, gave the unions access and influence that their counterparts in America didn't have. In short, airline unions in Europe have historically been much more influential in the overall development of the industry than in the United States. The airline unions have also been much more apt to call for strikes when their interests are threatened. It is a big part of the cultural legacy of the European system.

As big European airlines have been facing the same problems as the American carriers in recent years (high fuel prices, security concerns, growing budget carriers, overcapacity, little or no profits), their employees, unlike the American unions, have been more than willing to use the weapon of the strike to reassert themselves. In the eighteen months from the beginning of 2010 though the first half of 2011, European passengers and shippers endured numerous employee walkouts at Air France-KLM; a cabin crew strike at British Airways; a strike by mechanics at Air France; a walkout by pilots, flight attendants, and baggage handlers at Alitalia; a strike by pilots at Lufthansa; and, more than three dozen other shutdowns by the airline unions.[24] Further, as air traffic controllers unions across Europe are trying to block the advancement of a single air traffic control system for the EU, which would lead to lay-offs for the controllers, many of their fellow travelers in the airline unions regularly engage in slowdowns as signs of solidarity. If you fly often in Europe, like I do, you're wise to always check who is on currently on strike or threatening to go out before you leave home. Conversely, in the United States, during the same period of time, there were no strikes or similar actions by the airline unions.

All of this activity in Europe is being driven by the European airlines' effort to restructure their troubled industry. Not surprisingly, the unions are hitting back after years of cutbacks. The showdowns with unions come as European airlines, hurt by falling revenue and an uncertain economic outlook on the Continent, have taken a hard line on costs, including layoffs that have affected hundreds of thousands of workers since 9/11. The formerly state-run airlines are now competing with nimbler Flying Cheap rivals like

---

[24] Compiled from various media reports.

Ryanair and easyJet in their regional businesses, while battling Middle Eastern and Asian carriers for intercontinental traffic.

Further, while the U.S. experienced a greater negative impact from the crisis of 2008 than Europe in terms of bigger job losses and greater loss of wealth, it is the Europeans who have been markedly more animated about the fallout. Demonstrations across the Continent have been intense and long lasting. At the forefront of this civil disobedience are the unions. It seems many in Europe have learned what only a few in America have: the gains that workers used to be able to win through the unions have proved to be temporary. And airline unions now face new challenges no less implacable than their employers.

But the Industry is Hiring, and Hiring Big!

The nearly mature airline markets of the United States and European Union will not be centers of well-paying jobs moving forward and the unions will be further weakened through attrition. As the Flying Cheap strategy continues to take hold, retirees will be replaced with lower-paid workers and the airlines will constantly seek to do more with less. Most of the new hiring will be done at the low-paying, low-cost carriers where growth is expected to stay high.

In high-growth emerging markets, however, as the demand for air travel continues to rise, so will the need for airline workers. In fact, when it comes to airline pilots, the industry may very well be on the verge of what will be the biggest surge in pilot hiring in history. Forecasts realistically see a need for nearly 500,000 more commercial pilots by 2030, around 23,000 a year.[25] Nearly 40 percent of the openings will be in the soaring travel market in the Asia-Pacific region. The region will need 180,600 pilots in the next two decades, 70,600 for China alone.[26] Of course, pay levels will be a lot less for pilots there than it has been in American and the EU. Currently, the average German pilot earns more than $9,000 per month; the average American $4,200. Contrast this with a typical pilot of a Chinese airliner who earns $761 a month.[27] Demand for mechanics, flight attendants, customer service agents, and other airline jobs will also soar in the emerging markets, with comparable levels of pay.

---

[25] Charisse Jones, "World Demand for Pilots Expected to Soar," *USA Today*, June 26, 2011, http://www.usatoday.com/NEWS/usaedition/2011-06-21-Airline-pilots-1A-cover_CV_U.htm.

[26] Ibid.

[27] These are the latest figures for 2005 in current US dollars. www.worldsalaries.org/airlinepilot.shtml.

One Other Possible Threat to Airline Workers on the Horizon

With the airline industries in the U.S and EU seeking stabilization through the cost-cutting Flying Cheap strategy, there is also the threat of cross-Atlantic mergers and acquisitions. While American carriers can't presently merge with their European counterparts, and vice versa, this might be an option moving forward. Of course, it would require large governmental efforts to make the scenario palatable. If it were to occur, you can be certain that more jobs would be lost and remaining employees further squeezed.

The Future Is Now

The Planes of Tomorrow

"If it moves, tax it. If it keeps moving, regulate it. And if it stops moving, subsidize it."

—Ronald Reagan, on how government keeps expanding

The overarching themes involved in the manufacturing of aircraft today are the same ones that have dominated the entire airline industry since its inception. Think about it this way: the airlines are the customers who ultimately purchase the planes. We know how unprofitable the airlines are and how historically unstable the industry has been. So how is it that manufacturers, with all of their massive overhead and fixed costs, can sustain themselves when their customers are some of the least profitable companies in history? It's simple: the building of planes has been always been dependent on government subsidies and support for its survival. This is not a criticism, merely a statement of the way it is.

On the positive side of the ledger, the government's underwriting of aircraft manufacturing has been one of the great catalysts in moving the airline industry forward—opening up air travel for more and more people as aircraft have become more efficient, safer, and, ultimately, cheaper to operate. This ability to reduce costs is the most significant part of a human innovation.

When access to something becomes cheaper, more people can use it and benefit from it.

Going forward, new technologies and aircraft designs will dramatically change the operational environment of the industry going forward. I'm not yet ready to say this will lead to a period of long-term profitability for the airlines. That's a big stretch. Still, because of the introduction of better aircraft in the years to come, there will be a much more stable airline industry in the near future—a big reason for the soft landing, if you will.

The Coke and Pepsi of Commercial Aviation

Aircraft manufacturing is dominated by two mega-firms: America's Boeing and Europe's Airbus. These two firms constitute a duopoly. From the world of economics, a *duopoly* is when two firms control a given market. Like Coke and Pepsi in soft drinks, FedEx and UPS in package delivery, and AT&T and Verizon in mobile telecommunications, Boeing and Airbus dominate their industry. This is not to say that there aren't other companies who manufacture planes for the airline industry. Canada's Bombardier, Brazil's Embraer, and China's Commercial Aircraft Corp. are players, but they are currently marginal ones at best. Today and into the near future, the structure and direction for building and selling commercial aircraft will be determined by the two big boys. Many estimates conservatively project that global commercial aircraft sales will total more than $4 trillion in the next 20 years.

No single company has come to be identified with aviation more than Boeing. Founded by William Boeing, a wealthy Seattle resident who liked to fly, the company was one of many that tried to figure out the future of air travel during and after World War I. Virtually unknown except in the Pacific Northwest, Boeing hung around as a small firm until World War II, which changed everything. It was the Three Bs—the B-17, the B-29, and later, the B-52—that catapulted Boeing into one of the most important organizations in human history. Sheltered from market forces, competition, and the need to advertise and sell thanks to long-term, incredibly profitable Pentagon contracts, Boeing was able to evolve into an incredibly innovative, high-tech aircraft manufacturing giant.[1] Boeing leveraged the military contracts and additional governmental subsidies into a whole new division surrounding commercial aircraft, most importantly manufacturing the 700 series. These

---

[1] Bruce Cumings, *Dominion From Sea to Sea,* (New Haven, CT: Yale University Press, 2009), p. 364.

range from the innovative 707 to the workhorse 727 and the 737, the be-hemoth 747, and the sleek 787 "Dreamliner" that is scheduled to come on-line soon. Each of these aircraft has marked a distinctive step forward for the airline industry. The 707 was conceived in 1952 when Pentagon con-tracts for the Korean War were rolling in. When it finally appeared in 1959, the 707 seemed a generation ahead of any other airliner—and it was.[2] Big orders followed. The achievement of the 707 was surpassed by the incredi-ble success of the 747 in the 1970s and, later, the staples of the industry, the 727 and 737. Boeing was also well served by Senator Henry "Scoop" Jackson, who was often called the "the senator from Boeing" and was fa-mous for funneling huge amounts of federal money to the company.[3]

As testament to the company's global reach, China has become such a huge customer that Deng Xiaoping and Hu Jintao have both visited Boeing's as-sembly plant in Everett, Washington. When President Hu showed up in 2006, he donned a Boeing baseball cap during his tour. The love between China and Boeing is not surprising, as the Communists have purchased nearly 700 planes at a cost of more than $40 billion since 1972.[4]

Airbus was born in July, 1967 when government representatives from France, West Germany, and Britain agreed, "for the purpose of strengthen-ing European co-operation in the field of aviation technology and thereby promoting economic and technological progress in Europe, to take appro-priate measures for the joint development and production of an airbus."[5] This notion of collaboration in aviation was a byproduct of the greater po-litical and diplomatic integration that had started after World War II in Europe. Having been invaded and occupied by the Germans three times in 70 years, the French finally figured out it might be better to work with their neighbors to the east rather than fight them and lose again. In 1969, the French transport minister sat down with the German economics minister in a mock-up of the cabin of a new aircraft. The two politicians then signed an agreement officially launching the A300, the world's first twin-engine wide-body passenger jet. It was to be built by a French-German consortium that would also involve the British and the Dutch. The decision to give the go-ahead to the A300 was the formal starting point of the Airbus program.[6]

---

[2] Ibid.

[3] Cumings, p. 365.

[4] Cumings, p. 366.

[5] Airbus.com, "The success story of Airbus," www.airbus.com/company/history/the-narrative/early-days-1967-1969/.

[6] Ibid.

An element of Airbus' policy right from the start has been not to incorporate new technologies for their own sake but to carefully select meaningful applications that produce clear payoffs in safety, operational capability, and profitability benefits. This approach enabled the A300, when it entered service, to offer airlines a 20 percent savings in direct operating costs per trip relative to the competing jets. Another factor contributed to the growing recognition among airlines that the A300 offered valuable economic advantages over its rivals: not only did having one less engine considerably reduce the capital cost involved in buying the aircraft, but the A300's fuel efficiency became increasingly important as the 1973 oil crisis began to bite and prices soared.[7]

At the 2011 Paris Air Show, Boeing and Airbus carried the day as usual. Held every two years at Le Bourget Airport, where Charles Lindbergh landed on his famous non-stop transatlantic flight in 1929, the Paris Air Show is *the* place where the world's buyers and sellers get together to do deals. The sales by Airbus and Boeing dwarfed the competition and illustrated the present stranglehold the two companies have on the market for commercial aviation, as shown in Table 9-1.

Table 9-1. Commercial Aircraft Sales at the 2011 Paris Air Show. Source: Compiled from various media reports.

Manufacturer	Model	Quantity Sold
Airbus	A320neo	755
	A320	63
	A319neo	40
	A321neo	22
	A330	15
	A380	12
	A350	6
	A321	1
	Total	914

[7] Ibid.

Manufacturer	Model	Quantity Sold
Boeing	737	87
	777	27
	747	19
	787	4
	767	1
	Total	**138**
Embraer	**E190**	**39**
	Total	**39**
Bombardier	CS100	20
	CS300	10
	Total	**30**

Pots Call Kettles Black

As noted, the ability of Boeing and Airbus to keep any serious competition at bay has been rooted in the huge amounts of governmental subsidies they are each able to extract. Building the components for and assembling a commercial airplane is an incredibly complicated, time-consuming, and labor-intensive activity. For example, to manufacture and assemble a jet engine takes about two years—and that's after a design and testing period that can take up to five years for each model. The research and development phase is so protracted because the engines are so complex: a standard Boeing 747 engine contains almost 25,000 parts. To be able to survive the inherent convulsions that define the airline industry, while at the same time performing the necessary day-to-day functions to build an airliner, aircraft manufacturers and their suppliers have to be able to count on government to keep the road smooth when the inevitable potholes appear.

In a battle that seems to be never-ending, Airbus and Boeing regularly accuse each other of receiving illegal government subsidies. The fundamental point about this battle is that it's no big secret that these two aerospace giants depend on government to bring to market almost all of their products. Without government's support, neither would exist in its current form. Allan McArtor, head of Airbus's Americas office, described the situation aptly when he observed: "Boeing and Airbus both receive substantial government support, but they are decidedly different mechanisms and formulas. And it's a little bit like trying to balance baseball and cricket. They're kind of alike, but they're just different."[8] Although each company feeds at the governmental trough, the way they eat and even what they eat is not the same. Still, they would starve without government.

So, besides the aircraft themselves, what else do we get in return for all of this largesse? Boeing, Airbus, and all of their sub-contractors constitute some of the biggest private-sector employers in the world. Boeing's 747-40 has six million parts, 171 miles of wiring, and 5 miles of tubing. It consists of 147,000 pounds of high-strength aluminum. The design, sourcing, machining, fabrication, quality control, installation, and testing of all of this require an army of highly skilled (and highly paid) people. Boeing uses over 1,600 outside suppliers and sub-contractors on the plane. The continued existence of Boeing and Airbus guarantee good jobs for the communities and countries where they operate. To keep those jobs going, politicians are willing to throw big subsidies their way. Jobs mean campaign contribution and votes—the mother's milk of politics.

The current version of the "they get more subsidies than we do" fight began in 2004 and has made its way through numerous rounds of World Trade Organization (WTO) arguments and counter-arguments. The WTO is intended to be the final decider in disputes between international companies. It calls itself "the only global international organization dealing with the rules of trade between nations. At its heart are the WTO agreements, negotiated and signed by the bulk of the world's trading nations and ratified in their parliaments. The goal is to help producers of goods and services, exporters, and importers conduct their business."[9]

The first ruling said that Airbus received unfair government funding in the form of "launch aid" to build its commercial aircraft. According to the WTO, that funding led to a significant shift in market share away from Boeing. The United States, on behalf of Boeing, argued that the money given to Airbus qualifies as an illegal subsidy because the aerospace manufacturer is

---

[8] Adam Davidson, "Boeing, Airbus Subsidy Dispute Escalates," National Public Radio, May 31, 2005, www.npr.org/templates/story/story.php?storyId=4673068.

[9] World Trade Organization, www.wto.org/english/thewto_e/whatis_e/whatis_e.htm.

only required to pay back the "launch aid" if the plane succeeds in the marketplace. Meanwhile, Airbus argued that the tax breaks and funding from NASA and the Department of Defense give Boeing just as much of an advantage. In May of 2010, Airbus released a report claiming the following:

- Approximately $16.6 billion in government research and development subsidies to Boeing between the late 1980s and 2006, compared to an alleged $3.7 billion in research and development funding given to Airbus.
- Some $4.9 billion in state and local tax breaks granted to Boeing. (The figure didn't include newer tax breaks offered by South Carolina to Boeing.)
- A $1.5 billion injection from the Japanese government and close to $600 million from Italy toward production of Boeing's 787 Dreamliner, which would result in jobs moving overseas.[10]

In mid-September 2010, the WTO came back with an interim ruling responding to the claims made by Airbus. The trade referee's findings said that money supplied to Boeing through the Department of Defense and NASA constituted illegal taxpayer aid. Not included in the Airbus report about Boeing was the large amount of benefits the American firm is currently receiving from President Obama's National Export Initiative. Designed to jump-start exports coming out of the economic meltdown of 2008-09, the heart of the initiative is accelerating the activity of the Export-Import Bank, a government agency that subsidizes U.S. exports. "Ex-Im" lends money directly to foreign companies or governments—or guarantees private bank loans—so that foreign buyers will buy American-made products. Calling Ex-Im "corporate welfare" isn't a slur—it's a description.[11] The White House bragged that by the end of 2010, "Ex-Im had more than doubled its loans to support American exporters from the same period last year." They included a federal guarantee for JP Morgan to subsidize a Boeing aircraft sale to Turkey's Pegasus Airlines; another loan guarantee for Boeing to sell jets to Asiana Airlines; and, yet another Boeing subsidy guaranteeing jet sales to Nigeria.[12] In 2010, Ex-Im dedicated 64 percent of all its loans and long-term guarantees to subsidize Boeing sales.

---

[10] The Airbus report is entitled "Boeing Subsidies Report" and is dated May 26, 2010.

[11] Timothy Carney, "Boeing gets big tailwind from subsidized bank," *Washington Examiner*, March 10, 2010, http://washingtonexaminer.com/politics/boeing-gets-big-tailwind-subsidized-bank.

[12] Ibid.

Coincidentally, the Chairman of the President's Export Council is none other than Jim McNerney, CEO of Boeing. It probably makes some sense that the nation's largest exporter should hold this seat—and pocket most export subsidies—but this just goes to show why increasing government tends to benefit the biggest businesses. If there were no Ex-Im and no President's Export Council, Boeing's size wouldn't be so advantageous. McNerney expressed his confidence that Obama's council will advance policies to "expand free and fair trade." Of course, "free trade," when spoken by a politician, lobbyist, or CEO really means "subsidized trade."[13]

Of the companies outside of the duopoly, many assume that China will ultimately be able to manufacture aircraft on the scale of Boeing and Airbus, and that China's industrial might will continue to expand to the level of the First World. Through heavy subsidies to both local and international firms, price cutting, the encouragement of joint ventures, and even corporate espionage, China has sought to replicate what has been going on in aircraft manufacturing in Europe and the U.S. Of course, the mere existence of a Chinese aircraft manufacturing program is hyped by Boeing and Airbus as a way to secure more support from their local governments. It may very well take a few decades for China's manufacturing and technological infrastructure to develop to a point where it can truly compete against the West when it comes to airliners. Nevertheless, as traffic in Asia surpasses 30 percent of all global air-travel in the next few years, there may come a moment sooner than later when China is able to leapfrog into the mix.

The Future Is Now

We're told necessity is the mother of invention. A decade ago, jet fuel accounted for 15 percent of an airline's operating budget. Today, it's 35 percent.[14] This may seem contrarian, as planes and their engines have become much more fuel efficient in recent years, reducing the overall amount of fuel consumption. The rise in the percentage of the industry's total costs tied to fuel usage is a result of the cost-cutting strategies in other segments derived from the Flying Cheap strategy and the reduction in employee salaries and benefits. But in one of those crazy quirks of economics, the lowering of costs in some areas has made fuel a bigger component of the overall cost structure of the industry.

---

[13] Ibid.

[14] "Jets are becoming more efficient, saving fuel, money," *Associated Press*, July 5, 2011, www.stltoday.com/business/local/article_3822ef13-18b1-59cd-8119-3f5f9a13c61f.html#ixzz1RGBtk8DA.

This rise in dependency on fuel has been accompanied by concerns within the industry that it will need to reduce its carbon footprint in the coming years or face stiff penalties. As a result, aircraft manufacturers, facing pressure from their customers, are looking to squeeze every drop of inefficiency out of their planes. Airlines are so conscious of this that American is replacing its 19,000 catering carts with models that weigh 16 pounds less. Southwest is testing seat covers made with lighter fabric. JetBlue chose thinner seats for its new A-320s.

What about innovative new airplane designs that will make obsolete—even laughable—the workhorse planes we'll be flying for the foreseeable future? The vast majority of predictions about the future are at best interesting, most often useless, and maybe even treacherous. Next time you're surfing the Web, do a Google search for the "airplanes of the future." Story after story will present amazing, futuristic versions of wild and wacky aircraft that only the most imaginative among us can foresee. Prognostications are made about commercial aircraft that will fly at supersonic speeds around the world in 2.5 hours, or new designs that will make flying in economy class more luxurious. New models and technologies will lead to a better "[insert your fondest dream]."

For those of us old enough to remember, the Concorde was *the* future of air travel. Heralded in the 1970s as a revolution, the aircraft flew at twice the speed of sound—about 1,350 mph. While the average travel time between New York and London is about 7 hours, the Concorde could do it in around 3.5. For more than 20 years, the Concorde was held up as the way forward. But, because of its high costs to operate and maintain, as well as the incredibly expensive price for a ticket, it never fully got off the ground.

I actually flew it once, from London to New York on British Airways in 1996. I remember the take-off was pretty cool, as we got up faster than any commercial flight I've taken before or since. Inside, I remember being cramped. I am a pretty big guy and my 1996 frame was clearly not part of the original design plans from a few decades earlier. Arriving 5 or so hours earlier into JFK than normal was nice, but given the huge price difference between a ticket on the Concorde and one on a regular commercial flight, I never considered flying the Concorde again. Given the current trajectory of the airline industry and its embrace of the Flying Cheap strategy, we will most likely be flying in "new" versions of present day airplanes that will be remarkably similar to what the average passenger experiences today. The real improvements in aircraft will be in reducing costs and pollution—things we don't normally see as travelers.

Reducing the High Impact of Fuel Costs

Like so much of the transportation sector, the price of oil determines whether the airlines can turn a profit or not. The problem when it comes to fuel costs is that the airlines can't control the price. Instead, they are almost completely at the whims of global markets forces that ultimately determine how much a gallon of aviation fuel will cost. Aviation fuel is a specialized type of petroleum-based fuel used to power aircraft. It is generally of a higher quality than fuels used in less critical applications, such as heating or road transport, and often contains additives to reduce the risk of icing or explosion due to high temperatures, among other properties. Alcohol, alcohol mixtures, and other alternative fuels may be used experimentally, but alcohol is not permitted in any certified aviation fuel specification.

Lost in much of the concern about the recent rise of oil prices is the commodity's relationship to the weak U.S. dollar. Certainly political events in the Middle East and the potential of a serious supply disruption are factors influencing the short-term price of oil. Still, we often forget that the value of the greenback is historically the single greatest determinant. The dollar and oil have been inexorably linked since the 1920s when the "Seven Sisters" established the global oil business on the Arabian Peninsula. It's no coincidence that oil today is priced in dollars and, despite the metric system's widespread use around the world, still measured in 42 *gallon* barrels. This is the way the Seven Sisters—almost all of them U.S. oil companies—wanted it. The most recent rounds of quantitative easing by the Fed and concerns over growing governmental deficits in the U.S. have folks around the world spooked about the dollar's vitality. As evidence, the dollar was weaker relative to every other major currency throughout 2011. If you want to know where oil is headed, be sure to keep an eye on events in the Middle East and other volatile parts of the world—but, more importantly, follow the dollar.

Pressured by airline executives for improvements because of the uncertainty surrounding oil prices, manufacturers have pushed the frontiers of technology by building lighter planes and borrowing essential engine-design advances, such as automatic transmissions, from the auto industry. Airplane manufacturers have already reduced fuel consumption twice as much as car and train manufacturers have. In 1980, it took an average of 46 gallons of fuel to fly a passenger 1,000 miles. Today, it takes 22 gallons. Experts say the coming improvements could bring that number below 18 within a decade. That can't come soon enough for airlines struggling with the rising price of oil.[15] A $1 rise in the price of a barrel of oil adds to $1.6 billion in additional

---

[15] Ibid.

costs to the industry. In 2010, when oil prices were relatively low, the industry's net profits were $18 billion: a rare good year. In 2011, as oil prices continued to rise, the forecast for profits was only $4 billion.[16]

In the past few years, aircraft have been built out of the same lightweight materials used for Formula I race cars. Their engines have been redesigned to squeeze more thrust out of every bit of fuel. These and other advances have positioned airlines for the biggest gains in fuel efficiency since the dawn of the jet age in 1958. For airlines, more efficient jets will reduce their biggest expense. For passengers, it means fares may not jump around as much with the price of oil. "We're seeing 25 years of improvements compressed into 10 years," says Hans Weber, president of TECOP International, an aviation consulting firm.[17] The first Boeing 737, for example, was launched in 1967 and could carry about 100 passengers 1,725 miles. The most modern version, the B737-800, can carry nearly twice as many passengers twice the distance, while burning 23 percent less fuel.[18] Of the two major manufacturers, though, it is Airbus that is apparently winning the efficiently battle. Late in 2010, Airbus brought out a new version of its widely popular A320, the A320neo, that offers fuel savings up to 15 percent. It has become the fastest selling commercial aircraft in history, as evidenced by the more than 700 that were ordered at the 2011 Paris Air Show.

Shrinking the Industry's Carbon Footprint

As inflated worries over *global warming*—or is it now called *climate change* or *climate disruption?*—continue to persist, the industry, whether it likes it or not, is facing the very real threat of having to reduce the amount of pollution it produces. Estimates from the true believers hold that aviation is a relatively small but growing contributor to whatever is changing the weather: somewhere around 12 percent of all the carbon dioxide is emitted by the global transportation sector.

Starting in 2012, the European Union intends to tax flights coming in and out of Europe, as well as those within it, under the guise of the European Union's Emission Trading Scheme (ETS). Foreign carriers with European

---

[16] International Air Transport Association (IATA), "Forecast for 2011," www.iata.org.

[17] Ibid.

[18] "The aircraft of the future: plane truths," *The Economist*, March 12, 2011, p. 93

routes will face additional costs pegged to their fuel consumption when the EU begins limiting how much carbon dioxide airlines are allowed to emit before paying a penalty. The restrictions are expected to cost airlines worldwide $3.3 billion a year.

The U.S, China, and other nations are fighting the law in European courts. With billions of dollars of aircraft and engine orders at stake, manufacturers are turning designs that were dreams only a few years ago into reality. Boeing and Airbus are both building long-range jets—the 787 Dreamliner and A350, respectively—with half of their bodies made of carbon-fiber composites. The carbon-fiber weighs 20 percent less than traditional aluminum alloy.[19] But the real revolution in pollution reduction will come from the way planes are powered. Pratt & Whitney and CFM, a joint venture between General Electric and Safran, are announcing engines that promise to cut fuel use by 15 percent. These engines are designed for single-aisle planes, which account for more than 75 percent of the 22,000 jets worldwide. The engines should save more than $1 million per aircraft per year. "For the first time, we're seeing a propulsion horse race," says Richard Aboulafia, an analyst with the Teal Group.[20] Still, it may not be enough, especially for Airbus.

China, one of the biggest buyers of Airbus planes, is threatening to cancel any existing and future orders in response to the implementation of the ETS. For years, Airbus has sought to build better relations with the Chinese government. In 2009, it opened an assembly plant in Tianjin to tap the local market and build bridges with Chinese political leaders.[21] This is all in jeopardy, as China is objecting to what it sees as an illegal scheme to expropriate money from Chinese carriers. Airbus agrees and has asked the EU to reevaluate its stance. "A global issue needs a global solution," the company said in a letter to EU officials.[22] How this all plays out in the coming months and years will be testament to the power and influence of Airbus and its global customers. I think local economic interests will prevail.

The dominant control of aircraft manufacturing by the two major players will contribute in a significant way to the soft landing. The world's airlines will be able to count on new designs and improvements from Airbus and Boeing that are already underway. These are enabling the airlines to finally

---

[19] Ibid.

[20] "The aircraft of the future: plane truths," *The Economist*, March 12, 2011, p. 93

[21] Daniel Michaels, "China trips up major Airbus deal," *The Wall Street Journal*, Saturday/Sunday, June 25-26, 2011, p. B3.

[22] Ibid.

reduce their strong dependence on the cost of fuel, at least by enough to make a noticeable difference in the overall cost structure of the industry. By better getting their arms around the fuel issue, the airlines will have greater flexibility to manage other factors that will support its stabilization.

Infrastructure Spiffed?

Air Traffic Control, Airports, and Cargo

"Never discourage anyone...who continually makes progress, no matter how slow."

—Plato

The mention of the word "infrastructure" doesn't get a lot of people excited. It's not generally viewed as sexy and glamorous. In the context of the airline industry, the infrastructure is even more towards the back of the plane. Although air travel is no longer the thrilling adventure it used to be, the results of taking a flight often still are: the vacation of a lifetime; closing the big deal; seeing your son get married. Airports occupy a lot of our attention, but the behind-the-scenes activities like air traffic control (ATC) and cargo are mostly out of sight and mind. Unfortunately, it appears little will come from the infrastructure that will be game changers in the near term—except for maybe some improvements in the airport business model and a cleaning up of the terribly corrupt practices that have marred air cargo as of late. Still, given the importance of these elements in the day-to-day operations of the airline industry, they deserve our attention.

The First Airports

It was the U.S. Post Office Department that set the goal for a transcontinental airmail system between New York and San Francisco via Chicago by 1921. And it was under the leadership of the Post Office that local communities across America stepped up and built the real first airports. The next time you get on a flight, think about what it was like for passengers in the early 1920s. Weight was important on early aircraft because engines had only a small margin of lifting power, so passengers had to step onto scales to be weighed. If you were too big, there was no flight for you. If you survived the humiliation and passed the weight test, you would have to walk through the rain, snow, heat, or cold, and navigate rocks, mud, and dust to approach the already-running aircraft. Then, you would mount ladders and climb aboard. Many of the original "airports," which were little more than grass fields with some small buildings that served as rudimentary hangars and storage facilities, were part of the airmail system created in the United States just after World War I.[1]

As commercial air travel grew throughout the 1920s, the airlines began to introduce more passenger-friendly services and amenities. Before a flight, passengers might wait downtown at airline lounges and take an airline bus to the field just before departure. Universal Air Lines System, an airline of the late 1920s, built a downtown Chicago terminal with wicker furniture, a fireplace, and restaurant service.[2] While many across America were trying to promote air travel and its benefits, it was Charles Lindbergh's transatlantic solo flight across the Atlantic in 1927 that transformed the perception of aviation around the world. As an example, before Lindbergh's flight, Los Angeles leaders debated long and hard the necessity of building an airport. After the flight, L.A. began constructing a truly outstanding airport, Vail Field.[3] After World War II, airports—and their municipal owners—realized the need for larger terminals to accommodate more passengers and longer runways to handle bigger planes. 1959 was the first full year of U.S. commercial jet travel, and the first airport built specifically for the longer takeoff distances of jets was Washington Dulles.[4]

---

[1] Martin Greif, *The Airport Book, From Landing Field to Modern Terminal* (New York: Main Street Press, Mayflower Books, 1979).

[2] Robert Horonjeff and Francis McKelvey, *Planning & Design of Airports* (New York: McGraw-Hill Book Company, 1983).

[3] Alexander T. Wells, *Airport Planning & Management* (Blue Ridge Summit, PA: Tab Books, 1992).

[4] Ibid.

Transitions in the Current Airport Model

As the Jet Age marched forward through the second half of the 20ᵗʰ century, new airports were built and existing airports were expanded. Until recently, the business model for most airports in America was pretty simple: the owner—a governmental entity—would oversee and staff the airport. It would derive most of its income from the airlines, who would lease space for their operations and pay a fee for the right to take off and land there. The suppliers were the local governments and the airlines their customers. Passengers were widely viewed as the end users of the airport.

The hub-and-spoke system that the airlines expanded rapidly before and after deregulation became the mechanism for airports to find and secure new customers. Airport owners fought hard to convince an airline to locate a primary or secondary hub at their airport. And, once they got the airline to commit, the airport fought even harder to keep it. As airlines continued to experience the turmoil that is part of the industry's nature, including huge losses, bankruptcies, and mergers, airport owners would fill in the gaps and do all they could to ensure that their customers stayed put. This would include tax breaks, low cost loans, grants, and even direct cash injections to the airlines—all in the name of keeping the customer satisfied. The airports themselves were subsidized by the federal government, who poured (and continues to do so) billions into the construction and maintenance of America's airport infrastructure. It has been commonly estimated that the replacement cost of the current commercial airport system in the United States is more than $2 trillion—almost of all that is due to governmental spending at every level.

Moving forward, while it is clear that dependency on government funds for airports will remain, the nature of that dependency may be changing. You might think that means that privatization will be become more widespread. In fact, in 1997, Congress established the Airport Privatization Pilot Program (APPP) to explore privatization as a means of generating access to various sources of private capital for airport improvement and development. For the first time, private companies could own, manage, lease, and develop public airports.

The APPP authorized the FAA to permit up to five public airport sponsors to sell or lease an airport and to exempt the sponsor from certain federal requirements that could otherwise make privatization impractical. The airport owner or lease holder would be exempt from repayment of federal grants, return of property acquired with federal assistance, and the use of proceeds from the airport's sale or lease to be used exclusively for airport purposes. The pilot program began in September 1997.

On September 14, 2006, the City of Chicago submitted a preliminary application for Chicago Midway International Airport, a large hub airport.[5] The pilot program could only include one large hub airport, so applications for other large hub airports were to be placed on a standby list. As of October 25, 2010, there were only *four* active applications in the program and *none* on the standby list:

- Chicago Midway International Airport
- Gwinnett County Briscoe Field, Lawrenceville, Georgia
- Luís Muñoz Marín International Airport, San Juan, Puerto Rico
- Hendry County Airglades Airport, Clewiston, Florida[6]

So if we assume that privatization is a non-starter, how else might the business of airports be changing? For the first time, in order to expand their revenue streams because of the increasing uncertainty around government resources, airports have finally been beginning to treat passengers as customers, not just merely users of their facilities. You've probably already noticed this. Before 9/11, it was commonplace to arrive at an airport less than an hour before departure and navigate check-in, security, and then walk to the gate with plenty of time to spare. After 9/11, when security hassles mandated that passengers arrive a lot earlier prior to their flight, the airports began to realize they had a captive audience.

Some airports had experimented with the notion of having passengers spend more time—and money—with them well before 9/11. Pittsburgh International is one of America's newest major airports. It opened in 1992. The terminal was equipped with numerous innovative, state-of-the-art features at the time, including an AirMall with shops for passengers to spend money in. A "landside-airside" terminal eliminated the need for connecting passengers to go through security again. Unfortunately, Pittsburgh's strategy was a bit too forward thinking. As security expanded after the 9/11 attacks, passengers bypassed Pittsburgh's AirMall in the rush to get through the checkpoints and on to their gates.

Still, in the decade after the creation of the TSA and the new aviation security regimen, airports have begun to take advantage of some of their inherent

---

[5] FAA Airport Privatization Pilot Program, www.faa.gov/airports/airport_compliance/privatization/.

[6] Ibid.

strengths when it comes to the services they now offer passengers. Somewhere between 20 to 40 million passengers travel through a major commercial airport each year. Compare this with a large shopping mall in a prosperous locale, where 10 to 15 million visitors annually may visit. Further, people are spending more time in airports because they arrive earlier in order to have enough time to get through the security process. The mantra of "location, location, location" applies as much to airports as to any other property, and stores situated beyond security checkpoints are more desirable than those outside secure zones. Going forward, passengers will continue to see more high-end retail locations in airports, along with better restaurants, bars, and amenities like spas and salons. Also, there is a trend for airports to install their own passenger lounges—like airline clubs—that offer a relaxing environment as well as the facilities to do work, which today's traveling nomads require. All of this will be driven by the desire of airports to enhance their revenues through more offerings to passengers.

Air Traffic Control and Navigation: A Brief History in the U.S.

Air traffic navigation and control have been governmental responsibilities from the early days of air travel. Before the current system was created, automobile road maps and visual landmarks served as navigation aids for the early pilots. Sticking their head out the window was fine during the day, but at night they couldn't see anything. As airmail service began to take off after World War I, increasing demand required innovations to make night flying possible. In February 1921, an airmail pilot named Jack Knight flew all night from Chicago to North Platte, Nebraska. Knight found his way across the dark prairie with the help of bonfires lit by Post Office staff, farmers, and the public.[7]

By 1923, the Post Office had completed a transcontinental airway of beacons on towers spaced 15 to 25 miles apart, each with enough brightness to be seen for 40 miles in clear weather. On July 1, 1924, postal authorities began regularly scheduled night operations over parts of this route. By June 1927, 4,121 miles of airways had lights. By 1933, 18,000 miles of airway and 1,500 beacons were in place.[8] The towers all had numbers painted on them

---

[7] Roger E. Bilstein, *Flight in America, From the Wrights to the Astronauts*, Revised Edition (Baltimore: Johns Hopkins University Press, 1994).

[8] Nick A. Komons, *Bonfires to Beacons: Federal Civil Aviation Policy Under the Air Commerce Act, 1926-1938* (Washington, DC: DOT/FAA, 1980).

so they could be seen during the day. At night, the beacons flashed in a certain sequence so that pilots could match their location to a map they carried. The use of lighted airways allowed pilots to fly at night, but pilots still needed to stick their head out of the window to see the ground. It was becoming clear that was really needed was two-way voice communication.[9]

The Bureau of Standards began to work on two-way technology in December 1926 at its experimental station in College Park, Maryland. By the next April, it had an experimental ground-to-air radiotelephone system operating that could communicate up to 50 miles. Soon after, a transmitter installed at Bellefonte, Pennsylvania on the transcontinental airway successfully communicated with an airmail plane 150 miles away.[10] A radio navigation beacon was implemented in 1928, and, in 1929, Jimmy Doolittle became the first pilot to use only aircraft instrument guidance to take off, fly a set course, and land.

As more planes were taking to the skies, there was the growing fear of collisions on the ground and in the air. Traffic needed to be managed. In 1930, the first radio-equipped control tower in the United States began operating at the Cleveland Municipal Airport. By 1932, almost all airline aircraft were being equipped for radiotelephone communication, and about 20 radio control towers were operating by 1935. Further increases in flights created a need for air traffic control that was not just confined to airport areas but also extended out along the airways. In 1935, the principal airlines using the Chicago, Cleveland, and Newark airports agreed to coordinate the handling of airline traffic between those cities. In December, the first Airway Traffic Control Center opened in Newark, New Jersey. Additional centers in Chicago and Cleveland followed in 1936, the same year air traffic control officially became a federal responsibility.[11]

In the 1950s, air traffic control took a big leap forward with the introduction of radar into the system. In 1961, the FAA began using distance-measuring equipment. This equipment allowed aircraft to determine their distance from known checkpoints in order to confirm their position. In September 1964, the FAA instituted two layers of airways, one from 1,000 to 18,000 feet and the second from 18,000 to 45,000 feet. In October 1969, 16

---

[9] Ibid.

[10] Ibid.

[11] Glen A. Gilbert *Air Traffic Control: The Uncrowded Sky* (Washington, D.C.: Smithsonian Institution Press, 1973).

area navigation routes were developed. By the end of 1973, nearly 156 high-altitude area navigation routes were available.[12]

Waiting and Waiting for Progress

The last airway flight beacon from the system begun in the 1920s was shut down in 1973. And the air traffic control system has pretty much been stuck in 1973 ever since. While the relentless drive for greater efficiencies has taken firm root across much of the airline industry in recent years, one area that is seemingly still going boldly forth into the 1970s is air traffic control. Dishearteningly, the global positioning system in my golf cart probably has a more sophisticated guidance system than the domestic airliner I'm traveling in.

On a flight from say, Dulles to Chicago's Midway, the airliner will be handled by at least 10 air traffic controllers and their radar displays—at Dulles; Warrenton and Leesburg, Virginia; Indianapolis; Aurora and Elgin, Illinois; and Midway Airport. The limitations of the radar-based, 1950s-era system, which sweeps like the beam of a lighthouse, require the plane to fly miles out of its way and burn nearly 100 additional gallons of fuel. Because a jet plane can fly more than a mile and a half in the time it takes for that radar beam to come around again, the plane must be kept three to five miles from the nearest aircraft, which means there is more empty space in the skies than is needed and therefore more inefficiency—and higher operating costs—for the overall system.[13]

The very business of getting aloft (the time that passengers know as the minutes between the "buckle your seat belts" order and "you are free to move about the cabin") is an intricate choreography between controllers and the cockpit—and a highly inefficient one as well.[14]

On the flight from Dulles, just after liftoff, the pilot will repeat the compass direction given by the Dulles tower, letting the controllers know everything is OK. Then he tells a controller based in Warrenton that he's climbing. "Potomac departure, passing [1,800 feet] for 3,000, heading 270," he radios.

---

[12] Nick A. Komons, *Bonfires to Beacons: Federal Civil Aviation Policy Under the Air Commerce Act, 1926-1938* (Washington, D.C.: DOT/FAA, 1980).

[13] Ashley Halsey III, "New guidance system for skies could face delays," *Washington Post*, July 3, 2011, www.washingtonpost.com/local/antidote-to-air-gridlock-is-complex-undertaking/2011/06/30/AG9bdnwH_print.html.

[14] Ibid.

A new controller takes over and tells him to keep climbing to 5,000 feet and maintain that altitude. That keeps him 1,000 feet below flights heading to land at Dulles. When the plane reaches another waypoint, a third controller takes over and orders the flight to 12,000 feet. Over Linden, Virginia, the pilot is told to head for 17,000 feet. Then he is handed over to a fourth controller, operating on a different radio frequency, who takes the flight to 27,000 feet before handing over to yet another controller—the fifth—who ultimately guides the plane to its 40,000-foot cruising altitude. Now "you are free to move about the cabin."[15]

For nearly 40 years, the airline industry and its stakeholders have been looking for a new way forward when it comes to making air traffic control less complicated and more efficient. From a layperson's point of view, it may seem surprising that the system is stuck in the days of Nixon. One might ask, isn't progress inevitable? Haven't new computer technologies, mobile telephony, and global positioning systems been integrated over the years to make the air traffic control system more up-to-date and modern? The answer to each question, dishearteningly, is no.

Progress is not a constant nor is it always in the same direction. Sometimes it gets stale and sometimes it retards. The ancient Greeks and Romans had indoor plumbing and warm running water in many of their homes. The same style of living didn't reach the "modern" United States until our Civil War. The "antiquated" technology used by NASA to get the massive Saturn V rocket's cargo to the Moon and back has not yet been replicated. It is only the Saturn V—which was relegated to a premature retirement in 1972— that has transported human beings beyond low-earth orbit. This is not to say that there haven't been attempts to get the current air traffic control system out of the ditch and into the 21st century. There have been several tries that were, in the end, not much more than bandages to keep the old system functional. But today, it seems we might finally be on the verge of a big breakthrough.

The Next Generation Air Transportation Program (NextGen)

Many industry insiders in the U.S. are holding their breath that the revolution that is global positioning systems (GPS) will make its way into the practice of air traffic control. It is believed that by using GPS, NextGen will open

---

[15] Ibid.

up the skies that the present radar-based system is keeping closed. Using the same GPS precision that tells me how many yards I have to the center of the green, airplanes would be able to safely fly crowded skies at much closer distances. Moreover, they would be able to fly direct routes, unlike in the current system, which relies heavily on flying to waypoints before turning to a final destination. This ability to fly direct would save the airline industry billions in fuel costs and reduce its carbon footprint. In addition, it would permit a far more precise choreography of planes at airports, reducing the amount of fuel wasted while waiting for takeoff or languishing in holding patterns. For passengers, NextGen would cut flight delays, eliminate time spent on the runway waiting to take off, shorten the flight time once airborne, and bring fuel savings that promise to keep ticket prices lower.[16] All of this would create far greater efficiencies across the system and help to stabilize the airline industry. Everybody would win.

But before we get too excited here, let's remember that we are dealing with the historically contradictory environment that is the airline industry. Just because it seems like a good idea doesn't mean it can happen. The cost to implement the system is staggering. According to most estimates, it would be the biggest single investment in the history of civil aviation: somewhere around $45 billion over 10 years—divided roughly between the airlines and the FAA. It is believed this amount *should* be enough to cover the cost of replacement of the old system as well as the equipment, testing, deployment, and training of the new one—all while still safely managing 27,000 takeoffs and 27,000 landings every day. And there is that key word: *should*. Because it has never been done before, no one is sure what it might ultimately cost to make NextGen a reality, and that uncertainty has people scared to commit.

How Serious Is This?

Frankly, I don't have a lot of faith that NextGen will get started anytime soon. My lack of faith is attributable to that wise adage, "Follow the money." The U.S. Congress has already set some money aside for NextGen—somewhere around $1 billion for research and development. And a few of the airlines have stepped up, including Southwest, which has invested around $200 million to bring some of its planes and pilots up to speed, and Alaska Airlines, which is already using GPS precision landing procedures at Juneau International Airport. But supporters willing to put serious money

---

[16] Ibid.

where their mouths are remain few and far between. If there were ever a right time to fund NextGen, it would have been during President Obama's $700 billion stimulus package that was passed through the Congress in 2009 in the wake of the financial meltdown. The $20 billion or $45 billion or some other number for NextGen was not a big chunk of change relative to the total amount dedicated "to shovel-ready projects" and other economic stimulus projects. One wonders why not one dime was set aside from the $700 billion for NextGen, despite the many public pronouncements supporting the project over the years from both Presidents Obama and George W. Bush, as well as several key leaders in both political parties. It seems NextGen might be one of those Machiavellian items where politicians smile and promise they will do something about it every year, while, at the same time, doing everything they can behind the scenes to run away. NextGen appears to be far more valuable as an idea than it ever will be as a reality.

While the money has not flowed to NextGen, the FAA still has in place a deadline of 2020 for airlines to install key equipment that will tell controllers and other aircraft the location of their planes. But the agency has been slow to set technical standards and a deadline for other equipment necessary to realize the full benefits of NextGen.

Ironically, while America fidgets, the rest of the world seems to be looking to GPS as the wave of the future. The European Union is much further ahead in developing equipment standards for NextGen. As a result, the world may wind up adopting NextGen standards developed by the EU, rather than the United States. This would be a revolutionary shift, as the U.S. has been *the* standard for worldwide air traffic management since the inception of commercial air travel. And, even more discomforting, it was the U.S. government that developed GPS technology in the first place.

Air Cargo and the Airlines

Almost immediately after the introduction of the airplane, people were looking at ways to make it practical—and profitable. As passenger airlines sprouted up, the same companies also looked to add profits by filling up any available space with cargo. It made sense. Why not kill the proverbial two birds with one stone? If you're taking passengers across country, why not also carry a few bags of mail or something else that someone needs. As time went on, not surprisingly, passenger airliners also become large transporters of cargo for both government and private companies.

Moving cargo as well as passengers in the same aircraft provided the airlines with the opportunity to have multiple revenue streams to smooth over the inevitable rough patches innate to the industry. As a result, much of the history of air cargo in the United States is one of disappointment. While many entrepreneurs tried to enter the business and compete with the airlines for the movement of freight, they ultimately weren't successful. The airlines perceived "cargo-only" companies as threats to their own businesses and lobbied hard for the government to protect their interests. The airlines argued vociferously that any establishment of major air cargo companies would irrevocably damage passenger air travel. So, the CAA—the governmental entity in charge of the industry before deregulation and the one that set the rates and routes for air cargo—would almost always favor the airlines over the start-ups.

It was only until after deregulation that a new company was able to change the face of the air cargo business. A young entrepreneur named Fred Smith believed that combining passenger air traffic with freight air traffic, as the established airlines were doing, was not the most efficient way of doing business. He believed that the route patterns for the two were totally different. He also argued that combining freight with passenger traffic slowed down cargo delivery. Smith, with a lot of financial support, built a hub in Memphis, Tennessee, for his exclusive freight air delivery service, which he called Federal Express. One of the most important selling points was his idea of next-day delivery, a service that he guaranteed. The company began operations in April 1973 and while the initial years were financially difficult, by 1976, Federal Express was showing a profit. By 1982, the company had as many as 76 aircraft, including 39 Boeing 727s and four Douglas DC-10s. In 1983, the company reported revenues of $1 billion, an unheard of amount for a company that had existed for only ten years. In 1989, Federal Express acquired Tiger International, Inc. The two airlines merged in August 1989. As a result, Federal Express became the world's largest full-service all-cargo airline. In 1994, the company officially changed the name of its operating division to FedEx.[17]

United Parcel Service (UPS) is the other major player. The origins of UPS go back as early as 1907 to a bicycle-based delivery service. In its early years of operation, UPS primarily focused on contract service to retail stores. It was only in the 1950s that the company diversified into package delivery for a wide range of customers including private and commercial clients. UPS operated a short-lived air service beginning in 1929, but the

---

[17] T. A. Heppenheimer, *Turbulent Skies: The History of Commercial Aviation* (New York: John Wiley & Sons, 1995).

company began sustained air service via its UPS Blue Label Air much later in 1953. In the 1980s, UPS also expanded into international routes for documents and small packages.[18]

Holding On at All Costs

Today, the air cargo business is dominated by two kinds of companies: dedicated firms like FedEx and UPS and the airlines themselves. As FedEx and UPS continue to expand their presence both in the U.S. and around the world, the airlines are struggling to hold onto to their market share for cargo services. This was no more apparent than in the decade-long scandal that finally broke in 2011 in which airline executives from some of the world's largest carriers put together a massive price-fixing scheme to keep cargo fuel surcharges artificially high.

This conspiracy by many of the biggest airlines led to one of the largest criminal antitrust investigation in U.S. history. Between 2001 and 2006, when the global airline industry was reeling from the fallout of the 9/11 attacks, companies like British Airways, Korean Air, Air France-KLM, and others got together to fix the fees associated with cargo on flights coming to and from the United States. At the time of this writing, no U.S. carriers are known to be involved. Estimates say the airlines' crimes cost U.S. consumers and businesses hundreds of millions of dollars. To date, 19 executives have been charged with wrongdoing (four have gone to prison) and 21 airlines have coughed up more than $1.7 billion in fines.

The whole plot unraveled largely because two airlines decided to come clean and turn in their co-conspirators. In late 2005, officials from German-based Lufthansa notified the U.S. Justice Department that the airline had been conspiring to set cargo surcharges. By early 2006, FBI agents and their counterparts in Europe made the investigation public by raiding airline offices there. After those raids, British-based Virgin Atlantic came forward about its role in a similar scheme to set fuel surcharges for passengers. Investigators eventually found a detailed paper trail stretching back to 2000 that laid out agreements to set passenger and cargo fuel surcharges. The probe expanded to airlines doing business between the U.S. and Europe, Asia, South America, and Australia.[19]

---

[18] Ibid.

[19] Alicia A. Caldwell, "Airline Price Fixing Fines: Prosecutors Target 21 Companies Over Passenger, Cargo Fees," *Associated Press*, March 6, 2011, www.huffingtonpost.com/2011/03/07/airline-price-fixing-fine_n_832133.html?view=print.

Airlines and executives who didn't come forward were charged with violating the Sherman Antitrust Act. Two former airline executives were sentenced to six months in prison; two others were ordered to prison for eight months. Charges are pending against 15 executives, nine of whom are considered fugitives. Bruce McCaffrey, one-time vice president of freight for the Americas at the Australian carrier Qantas, pleaded guilty to conspiracy to restrain trade. He was sentenced to six months in prison in 2008. He admitted working with other airlines to fix cargo fuel surcharges between 2000 and 2006. Keith H. Packer, a former senior manager of sales and marketing for British Airways, pleaded guilty to conspiracy to restrain trade and was sentenced to eight months in prison in 2008. He admitted joining the cargo conspiracy in 2002 and participating until February 2006.

British Airways and Korean Air pleaded guilty to violating the Sherman Act; each was fined $300 million in August 2007.[20] British Airways admitted fixing cargo surcharges from 2002 to 2006 and passenger fuel surcharges from 2004 to 2006. Korean Air admitted fixing cargo and passenger surcharges from 2000 to 2006. As an example of the impact of the conspiracy, fuel surcharges imposed by some of the conspirators rose by as much as 1,000 percent during the conspiracy, far outpacing any percentage increases in fuel costs that existed during the same time period.[21]

While there are small cargo start-ups, the big gorillas in the industry will continue to garner most of the business. In fact, it seems the current shape of the infrastructure that supports the airline industry is stuck. There will be some improvements in the coming years, especially at airports where passenger convenience will become a top priority, but the big picture in the future will be quite similar to what we have had for the past decades. Innovation, if it comes, will be arduously slow.

---

[20] Ibid.

[21] Ibid.

Flying in Our Future

"Do I contradict myself? Very well, then, I contradict myself;
I am large—I contain multitudes."

—Walt Whitman

When put together, I believe the details in the previous chapters explain how the airline industry is set up for a soft landing. This is not an empirical conclusion. A system that is as complex and variable as the global airline industry is not best explained by statistical findings and conclusions. Sure, numbers can tell us a lot, like the overall size of industry losses, passenger load factors, etc. But how can we effectively measure intangibles like stability, personal convenience, and indispensability, as well as future—and unknown—economic and social benefits for individuals and humankind that come from more access to the system? The profound reach of the airline industry into our lives as passengers, consumers, taxpayers, and citizens deserves this and so much more. For these reasons, the case I've made here has been rooted in a qualitative evaluation of the relevant facts and evidence.

I am completely aware, however, that despite the tremendous advances in human knowledge, it is very difficult to definitively prove anything. We like to pretend that our analyses and experiments can define the truth for us.

But that is often not the case. Just because an idea is true doesn't mean that it can be proved. And just because an idea can be proved doesn't mean it's true. When all of the work is done on a given matter, we still have to choose what to believe.

Here, at my closing argument, the preponderance of what has been presented reveals that the airline industry is on the precipice of a new era in which stability is much more the norm than the exception, the inevitable turndowns are not as bad, and everyone associated with the industry has much clearer and realistic expectations of what the airlines can and cannot do for them. None of these should be dismissed or shrugged off.

Greater stability for the industry will immensely profit passengers and taxpayers—the same folks who ultimately underwrite so much of the costs of keeping the industry alive. Smoothing over some of the rough patches will enable governments to better plan and allocate where their support of the industry can be best targeted. And when it comes to clearer, more realistic expectations, everyone will end up saner and less flummoxed when things don't go as planned. As a critical component of our modern world, a much more robust and resilient airline industry will play an increasingly important role in expanding human interaction and exchange. Whether we use the system or not, all of us are better served by an airline industry that is healthy and on the right track.

So What Changes Should Passengers Expect Flying in Their Future?

The arrival of the soft landing has already provided a window into what passengers should anticipate going forward. Much of this is rooted in a more direct relationship with the airlines. Having effectively leveraged the Internet to remove the middlemen between themselves and their passengers, the airlines have been steadily getting closer to us. Whether it is saving our seating preferences—window or aisle—or keeping us regularly updated on new ticket deals when some load factors need a boost, the airlines are able to communicate with their customers in ways never before imagined. Furthermore, passengers have greater accessibility to the airlines as well. Genuine two-way relationships are developing.

More Access to the Airlines' Global Network

I used to make a lot of intra-Africa trips back in the 1990s. Checking available flights and booking a reservation was grueling, to say the least. My travel agent—God bless her—tried the best she could. In the days before the Internet, just trying to get a flight schedule between Ouagadougou and Bamako could take hours or even days. Buying a ticket from the U.S. for such a flight, even with a major credit card, was arduous—and risky as well. Today, anyone anywhere can simply log on to www.air-burkina.com and within seconds have access to the entire reservation system with all of the flight schedules readily available. For those who want to buy a ticket, it can be done securely in a few minutes. And, unlike the pre-Internet days where the paper tickets would have to be snail-mailed—another not-so-easy process—electronic ticketing today makes all of this unnecessary. In the long run, having more access to the global network of the airlines with all of that information saves passengers a huge amount of time and provides immense value. As advances in technology allow for new platforms and increased integration, passengers will one day soon have everything they need just a mouse click away.

More Product Offerings from the Airlines

Through this relationship-building process, the airlines are able to better expand their offerings to passengers, and provide additional products and services that enhance their bottom line. Maybe it's the discount on a rental car or a hotel room booked through the airline's web site or a vacation package to Hawaii. Whatever it is, the airlines are positioned to sell more travel-related products than just those they offered in the past. Airline credit card offerings are already providing benefits to travelers, such as early boarding, club access, free checked bags, and elite status. Auctions and cross-branding with non-travel companies are further opening up opportunities for passengers to get better deals across a wide spectrum of categories.

More Self-Service

From booking the ticket online, to using your own toner to print out the boarding pass, to using the kiosk machines in the terminal to check in, airline passengers are increasingly finding themselves to be their own customer service agents. Contact with representatives of the airline industry is becoming rare indeed. But this is really nothing new. For years, activities that were once highly serviced-focused and people-intensive have been outsourced to the customer themselves. On a normal evening drive home from the office, I can fill up the tank, wash my car, check a book out at the library, and get a few bucks from the ATM without ever having made contact with another human being. Add in all the services I can now accomplish at home through the Internet—not having to go to the Bureau of Motor Vehicles to renew my license plates is a big one for me—and it is easy to conclude that self-service is an important part of our lives. And it will continue to get more widespread. When the possibility arises to outsource more and more services to passengers, we should anticipate that the airlines are going to take full advantage of it.

More Charges for the Things You Do and Use

The unbundling of services through the Flying Cheap strategy has been such a winner for the airlines that we should expect to find more á la carte charges in the future. As the compulsion to better manage fuel costs becomes ever more intense, weight—of carry-ons, checked bags, and maybe even passengers—will move higher up the priority ladder. To handle this challenge, it becomes foreseeable that weight restrictions—and charges for exceeding them—could get even stiffer. Improved personal entertainment systems will provide new avenues for the airlines to introduce revenue streams within the cabin. Seating configurations will be tinkered with, too, as the airlines learn more about how many of their fliers are willing to pay extra for an aisle, emergency exit, or a seat closer to the front. Paperless will become the norm, and those folks who prefer a hard copy instead of a virtual alternative will likely pay for it. For those of us who are willing to endure the lowest form of customer treatment, the only benefits will be a cheap ticket and a seat—likely somewhere in the back of the plane and in the middle of the row. Anything else will almost certainly have an extra cost associated with it.

More Variety and Places to Spend Your Money at Airports

The realization by airports that they are more than mere transit stations is giving passengers a new array of options when it comes to shopping, unwinding, eating, and working. Airports are now dining spots, business centers, retail destinations, and relaxation points. In the U.S. and much of Europe, existing airports will continue to be reconfigured to adapt to this model. Expect lots of construction zones in the coming years. In the developing world, hundreds of new airports, large and small, will each be designed with the passenger fully in mind. The idea is to make passengers feel welcome and warm in the airport throughout their stay, so that they will ultimately be comfortable enough to spend some of their money there. Airports around the world should finally become strong revenue generators for the entities that own them.

A Simpler Image of What Air Travel Is

As the unstoppable march of time takes us further and further away from the days of the jet set, the confusion that has dominated much of the discussion about the air travel experience will fade. Anyone under the age of 40 only knows the flying experience for what it is today: cheap, cattle-class, like taking the bus. As the over-40 crowd continues to adjust their expectations to the shifts of the last two decades, a general agreement will evolve across the whole population of fliers regarding the image of air travel. It is already well underway and will get stronger going forward. Memories of Sunday-best clothes and complimentary champagne in economy class will remain just that: recollections of a long-ago era that has no chance of ever coming back. Instead, the consensus of air travel being a lot like going to Wal-Mart will more firmly take hold.

So What Won't Change Much?

While there are some notable changes on the horizon for passengers, it is remarkable how much is not expected to be different in the coming years. Bluntly stated, a good portion of the airline industry will still be all too familiar. This should not be viewed as uncommon nor a surprise. Human endeavors are constantly in motion, wavering somewhere between the status quo and rapid, accelerated change. Most of the time, different parts of complex systems find themselves in various locations on this spectrum. There are even times when things move backwards. Because of this reality, we should expect some portions of the airline industry to be experiencing a quicker pace of change than others.

The Continued Security Muddle

Aviation security is one of those areas where, unfortunately, things will stay close to the status quo. Neither politician, bureaucrat, nor most passengers want to see security look like it did on the morning of 9/11. It is stunning with how much ease the terrorists on that day were able to achieve their goals. No one can legitimately argue that the aviation security system put in place after 9/11 doesn't *look* more impressive. Whether it is actually any better, especially given the increased threat level the airline system now faces precisely because of the success of the 9/11 attacks, is another issue. What is certain is that the current strategy for managing aviation security is reactive—and responds only to what those who want to harm the system try to do. By always being one step behind the bad guys, aviation security will remain relegated to playing catch-up, with the true objective being an emotional appeal to fliers that everything is OK because it *looks* so. However, the problem one day will arise when the introduction of a terrorist tactic—like the body cavity bomb—will lead to the implementation of new security measures that might very well keep passengers away and seriously damage the soft landing. Currently, there is nothing in place to keep this chain of events from unfolding.

Delays and More Delays

The combination of the hub-and-spoke system and the antiquated radar-based air traffic control network, exacerbated by the near capacity of most already-existing airports, means that delays will remain common for the industry—and passengers. When piled on by bad weather and mechanical issues, the effects of a glitch can cascade rapidly throughout the system, forcing delays three or four degrees removed from where the problem originated. The just-in-time nature of the airline industry has to also recognize the real possibility of negative events rippling quickly across time zones.

Packed Planes

The ability of the airlines to better gain and manage customer data has been one of the big leaps forward in getting to the soft landing. Passenger Load Factors (PLFs) are at all-time highs and we should expect that this will remain the case into the future. By being able to keep flights near 80% full, while identifying the underperforming routes and either cancelling or cutting ticket prices to fill them, the airlines have finally gotten their arms around this challenge.

Remarkably Similar Aircraft

The recent introduction of Airbus' A-380 and Boeing's 787 Dreamliner have been hyped as game changers for the industry. While they may very well alter the cost structure of the airlines by lowering fuel usage and, therefore, total costs—which helps to underpin the soft landing—most passengers will still find themselves in a cattle class-type experience, regardless if the plane they are flying in is new or not. Moreover, most of the planes most of us will continue to fly in will continue to be the old workhorses of the industry, especially Boeing's 737.

The Lack of Consistent, Regular Profits

I have said throughout this book that the industry has never been able to enough profits to sustain it through the down years and keep it growing. If you recall, I went further and questioned whether airline industry is really an industry in the pure sense of the term. The origin of the air transport system was not driven by the insatiable need for things like economies of scale, profits, or return on investment. Over the history of commercial air travel, there have certainly been entrepreneurs who tried to shove the round peg into the square hole and make profits where there was little chance. A few succeeded, but most didn't. This in itself is not unique to any business venture. However, what separates the airline industry from other areas is the massive amount of government support the industry has received since its inception. Without it, there never would have been anything remotely similar to the expansive, affordable, and incredibly safe aviation sector we have today. If the industry had principally relied upon profits to make it happen—with maybe a fair amount government aid thrown in like a lot of "private" companies receive—the result would have been a miniscule system a fraction of the size it is today. Going forward, nothing in the soft landing points to a sudden burst of sustainable profits for the industry. If stability is wrongly interpreted as the formation of a new paradigm and industry leaders decide to make decisions as if they operating were in a normal business, things could turn sour in a hurry.

What Are the Potential Threats to the Soft Landing?

While the path to the soft landing appears to have opened up quite nicely, there are roadblocks that can slow it down or even knock it off course. Potential threats can come from two areas: those that could occur within the industry (internal) and those take place outside of it (external). From the big picture level, both internal and external threats to the soft landing would most likely stem from a reduction in the overall market size that the airlines serve. In other words, the number of passengers would get smaller over time. This is not the only threat, but it is the biggest.

Internal Threats

Internally, this could be driven by a substantial rise in ticket prices driven by greed. It may seem counterintuitive, but steady, low fares over the long-term may work against the industry's soft landing, if not handled correctly. It's hard to see how fares can go any lower than they currently are. As the airline industry stabilizes, there may be a strong temptation to raise fares. Greed is a powerful force. Shareholders, along with Wall Street analysts and the business press, have proven themselves to be very persuasive when it comes to convincing a CEO what to do.

Although no one quite knows for sure what it is, there does exist a threshold for most travelers in terms of how much they will pay for a ticket. The airlines shouldn't assume that the indispensability they enjoy in the minds of so many people today is a blank check to raise prices when they can. That dependency exists, in part, because of the low prices people expect to pay. It seems there is an equilibrium emerging between passengers and airlines as to what the range of fares should be. A significant deviation from this could jeopardize the soft landing.

Earlier in the book I did raise some concerns about the prospects of negative outcomes resulting from the industry's continued embrace of outsourcing. Critical functions like aircraft maintenance and safety can't be compromised at any time. The expansion of these activities beyond national borders, where the ability to monitor and control them is difficult, should raise red flags for everyone associated with the industry. Industry regulators and those who oversee them must stay vigilant and not allow the drive for greater efficiencies to compromise the incredible safety record the industry and its stakeholders enjoy. A failure to keep the flying public's safety as the number one priority is not an option.

The continued reduction in the wages and benefits of many airline employees, especially those in the U.S. and Europe, could one day backfire and stall the soft landing as well. Aggressive union action and widespread strikes to demand better pay and working conditions will be possibilities in the years ahead. The leaders in the industry will need to consistently reach out to their co-workers and explain what they are doing, and why, to insure that any conflicts are resolved fairly and smoothly before things spiral out of control. Not doing this will make it that much harder to maintain stability.

External Threats

Externally, the number of passengers could shrink due to rises in ticket prices that are forced upward not by greed, but by a sudden, dramatic spike of oil prices. With fuel costs being such a substantial portion of the overall operating expenses of the industry, an event that pushes the price of a barrel of oil into the stratosphere would suspend the soft landing indefinitely. I'm talking about $180 a barrel or higher for an extended period of time. Geopolitical uncertainty in the Middle East, which provides the world's economy with the largest amount of its oil, always keeps us anxious. Fears over an emerging Cold War—and maybe even a hot one—between Iran and Saudi Arabia are very real. Further, the prospect of a nuclear-armed Iran is something that appears unstoppable.

Beyond a rapid spike in oil prices always lies the possibility of a wider shock to the overall economy. This could have the same kind of impact as $180 a barrel oil. Also, chronic stagnation in the developed world could set back the soft landing a bit, although passengers around the world have continued to fly in significant numbers since most of the world entered the Great Recession in 2008. Fears of a global pandemic are not overblown and could also put a damper on things.

Another concern is that given the world's current fiscal problems, governments may feel the need to pull back on their historically high levels of support for the industry. If, instead of continued government backing, overtures are made to replace it with privatization and increased competition from abroad, fractures in the soft landing could occur. How? A key pillar in stabilizing the industry is the regular contributions from governments around the world. If that pillar, which has been very dependable over time, is removed, and replaced with the inherent instability that comes from market forces, the industry would fall back into its old ways very quickly.

Fortunately, the industry appears positioned to better deal with the external events than any time in the past. A major terrorist attack like 9/11 against the air transport system would certainly reverberate worldwide and cause a temporary slowdown. However, the fact that it would come more than 10 years after 9/11 would ultimately reduce its impact in the minds of passengers. The greater fear would be the predictable overreaction that officials would put in place to reassure the traveling public, which might ultimately erode the willingness of many passengers to deal with the security hassles of flying. This is illustrative that a good deal of maintaining the soft landing will be contingent upon decisions by leaders across the industry.

And the Winner is . . .

In other words, for the first time in memory, the majority of what shapes the airline industry will come from the inside, rather than out. As the soft landing takes hold, it will be up to the leaders of all the stakeholder groups—airline CEOs, manufacturing executives, government officials, union chiefs, passenger advocates, and more—to first recognize the opportunity brought about by the soft landing, and then work diligently to keep it in place. It has taken decades to arrive at this moment. To squander it now would be a travesty. History will remember the folks who facilitated the soft landing as well as those who fought against it.

So now we conclude our brief time together at the same place we started, with the thoughts of Voltaire, the author of the Enlightenment. Throughout this book, I've tried to stay true to his axiom that the enemy of good is perfection. That the present airline industry and the modern air travel experience—with all of the stresses and strains, imperfections and flaws—remain wonderful advantages for more and more of us each day.

Voltaire published his classic novel *Candide* in 1759. It is one of the best road trip stories ever. In it, young Candide wanders from his home in Westphalia and is captured by recruiters who impress him into service in the Bulgarian Army. He marches through deserts, battles, and faraway places. He eventually escapes the army, arrives shipwrecked into Lisbon, and is arrested by the Inquisition. He meets his new companion Cunegonde and they eventually flee Europe for the New World, hoping it will be less cruel than the Old.

In Buenos Aires, Cunegonde is taken as a concubine by the commandant there. Candide is banished and runs to Paraguay, before falling upon El Dorado in a secluded Peruvian valley. He picks up some gold and moves on, still hungering for his lost soul mate. He sails back to Europe and arrives in Portsmouth, where he learns that Cunegonde is in Venice. He goes there, only to discover she had already been sent to Constantinople. When they are finally reunited in the Turkish city, Cunegonde is now an old, ugly slave; nevertheless Candide frees her and marries her. Reunited at last, Candide and Cunegonde decide to till a small plot of ground and grow their own food, knowing that it is the best possible of all worlds, since their sufferings have brought them this peace: "*mais il faut cultiver notre jardin*" (we must cultivate our garden). The little story ends.

While Voltaire knew quite well that few men ever encounter so bitter a chain of catastrophes as Candide's, he must have also known that though it is good to cultivate one's garden, to live truly well is to have a greater appreciation for the world beyond our home. How fortunate are we today that to gain such an awareness is nearly as simple as going online, giving your credit card number, arriving at the airport, and then sitting back while the world magically opens itself up to us.

GAO Report on Aviation Security

I've included this 2010 report from the Government Accountability Office (GAO) to further demonstrate the current strategy TSA takes towards aviation security management. If you're not familiar with the GAO, it is an independent, nonpartisan agency that works for Congress. Often called the "Congressional watchdog," GAO investigates how the federal government spends taxpayer dollars.

As we saw earlier in the book, the focus of TSA has been overwhelmingly reactive when it comes to dealing with the ongoing threat posed by terrorists and criminals. That is, in order to keep passengers feeling safe when they fly, TSA responds with new security measures designed to prevent the last attack from reoccurring. This is why cockpit doors were reinforced *after* 9/11. Our shoes now must come off because of the shoe bomber's failed try in November 2001. Any liquid over 3.4 ounces is banned because of the discovery of a 2006 plot to disguise bombs in bottles of sport drinks. And now, we are all subjected to the naked X-ray machines due to the underwear bomber's attempt to blow himself up on Christmas Day 2009.

Words matter. Check out the introductory paragraph under the heading "TSA Plans to Procure and Deploy 1,800 AITs by 2014" and you'll get a good sense of why aviation security operates as it does:

> In *response* to the December 2009 attempted terrorist attack, TSA has revised its procurement and deployment strategy for the AITs [AITs are the naked X-ray machines], increasing the number of AITs it plans to procure and deploy. In contrast with its prior strategy, the agency now plans to acquire and deploy 1,800 AITs (instead of the 878 units had previously planned to acquire) and to use them as a primary screening measure where feasible rather than solely as a secondary screening measure. According to a senior TSA official, the agency is taking these actions in *response* to the Christmas Day 2009 terrorist incident. [Italics and brackets are mine.]

This current practice of reacting to the bad guys and then deploying a new widespread measure to stop the threat from repeating itself is not sustainable. As terrorist tactics become more innovative—including, but not limited to, bombs hidden within body cavities, breast implants, or other anatomical features—the present strategy will lead to a conclusion that would seriously harm the soft landing.

AVIATION SECURITY

TSA Is Increasing Procurement and Deployment of the Advanced Imaging Technology, but Challenges to This Effort and Other Areas of Aviation Security Remain
GAO-10-484T

Statement of Steve Lord, Director
Homeland Security and Justice Issues
United States Government Accountability Office

Testimony Before the Subcommittee on Transportation Security and Infrastructure Protection, Committee on Homeland Security, House of Representatives.

Why GAO Did This Study

The attempted bombing of Northwest flight 253 highlighted the importance of detecting improvised explosive devices on passengers.

This testimony focuses on (1) the Transportation Security Administration's (TSA) efforts to procure and deploy advanced imaging technology (AIT), and related challenges; and (2) TSA's efforts to strengthen screening procedures and technology in other areas of aviation security, and related challenges. This testimony is based on related products GAO issued from March 2009 through January 2010, selected updates conducted from December 2009 through March 2010 on the AIT procurement, and ongoing work on air cargo security. For the ongoing work and updates, GAO obtained information from the Department of Homeland Security (DHS) and TSA and interviewed senior TSA officials regarding air cargo security and the procurement, deployment, operational testing, and assessment of costs and benefits of the AIT.

What GAO Found

In response to the December 25, 2009, attempted attack on Northwest flight 253, TSA revised the AIT procurement and deployment strategy, increasing the planned deployment of AITs from 878 to 1,800 units and using AITs as a primary—instead of a secondary—screening measure where feasible; however, challenges remain. In October 2009, GAO reported on the challenges TSA faced deploying new technologies such as the explosives trace portal (ETP) without fully testing them in an operational environment, and recommended such testing prior to future deployments. TSA officials concurred and stated that, unlike the ETP, operational testing for the AIT was successfully completed late in 2009 before its deployment was fully initiated. While officials said AITs performed as well as physical pat downs in operational tests, it remains unclear whether the AIT would have detected the weapon used in the December 2009 incident based on the preliminary information GAO has received. GAO is verifying that TSA successfully completed operational testing of the AIT. In October 2009, GAO also recommended that TSA complete cost-benefit analyses for new passenger screening technologies. While TSA conducted a life-cycle cost estimate and an alternatives analysis for the AIT, it reported that it has not conducted a cost-benefit analysis of the original deployment strategy or the revised AIT deployment strategy, which proposes a more than twofold increase in the number of machines to be procured. GAO estimates increases in staffing costs alone due to doubling the number of AITs that TSA plans to deploy could add up to $2.4 billion over its expected service life. While GAO recognizes that TSA is attempting to address a vulnerability exposed by the December 2009 attempted attack, a cost-benefit analysis is important as it would help inform TSA's judgment about the optimal deployment strategy for the AITs, and how best to address this vulnerability considering all elements of the screening system.

TSA has also taken actions towards strengthening other areas of aviation security but continues to face challenges. For example, TSA has taken steps to meet the statutory mandate to screen 100 percent of air cargo transported on passenger aircraft by August 2010, including developing a program to share screening responsibilities across the air cargo supply chain. However, as GAO reported in March 2009, a number of challenges to this effort exist, including attracting participants to the TSA screening program, completing technology assessments, and overseeing additional entities that it expects to participate in the program. GAO is exploring these issues as part of an ongoing review of TSA's air cargo security program which GAO plans to issue later this year. Further, while TSA has taken a variety of actions to strengthen the security of commercial airports, GAO reported in September 2009 that TSA continues to face challenges in several areas, such as assessing risk and evaluating worker screening methods. In September 2009, GAO also recommended that TSA develop a national strategy to guide stakeholder efforts to strengthen airport perimeter and access control security, to which DHS concurred.

What GAO Recommends

GAO is not making new recommendations. In past reports, GAO has recommended, among other things, that TSA operationally test screening technologies prior to deployment and assess costs and benefits of screening technology investments. DHS concurred and is working to address the recommendations. DHS provided comments to this statement, which were incorporated.

Testimony

Madame Chairwoman and Members of the Subcommittee, I am pleased to be here today to discuss the Transportation Security Administration's (TSA) progress in securing passenger checkpoints and other areas of commercial aviation. In response to the December 25, 2009, attempted bombing of Northwest flight 253, the Secretary of Homeland Security announced five corrective actions to improve aviation security, including accelerating deployment of the advanced imaging technology (AIT)—formerly called the Whole Body Imager—to identify materials such as those used in the attempted Christmas Day bombing. The AITs produce an image of a passenger's body that TSA personnel use to look for anomalies, such as explosives. TSA is deploying AITs to airport passenger checkpoints to enhance its ability to detect explosive devices and other prohibited items on passengers. Passengers undergo either primary or secondary screening at these checkpoints. Primary screening is conducted on all airline passengers before they enter the sterile area of an airport and involves passengers walking through a metal detector and their carry-on items being subjected to X-ray screening.[1] Secondary screening is conducted on selected passengers and involves additional screening of both passengers and their carry-on items. While screening passengers at the checkpoint is a vital layer of security, it is also important to ensure the security of other areas of commercial aviation, such as air cargo transported on passenger aircraft, and airport worker screening and checked baggage screening.

TSA's passenger checkpoint screening system comprises three elements: (1) personnel responsible for, among other things, screening passengers and baggage; (2) the policies and procedures that govern the different aviation security programs; and (3) the technology used to screen passengers and baggage. All three elements—people, process, and technology—collectively help determine the effectiveness and efficiency of passenger checkpoint screening, and our past work in this area has addressed all three elements of the system.[2] Similarly, securing the flying public involves

---

[1] Sterile areas are areas of airports where passengers wait after screening to board departing aircraft.

[2] See for example, GAO, Homeland Security: Better Use of Terrorist Watchlist Information and Improvements in Deployment of Passenger Screening Checkpoint Technologies Could Further Strengthen Security, http://www.gao.gov/products/GAO-10-401T (Washington, D.C.: Jan. 27, 2010); Aviation Security: DHS and TSA Have Researched, Developed, and Begun Deploying Passenger Checkpoint Screening Technologies, but Continue to Face Challenges, http://www.gao.gov/products/GAO-10-128 (Washington, D.C.: Oct. 7, 2009); Homeland Security: DHS's Progress and Challenges in Key Areas of Maritime, Aviation, and Cybersecurity, http://www.gao.gov/products/GAO-10-106 (Washington, D.C.: Dec. 2, 2009); Aviation Security: TSA Has Completed Key Activities Associated with Implementing Secure Flight, but Additional Actions Are Needed to Mitigate Risks, http://www.gao.gov/products/GAO-09-292 (Washington, D.C.: May 13, 2009); Aviation Security: Preliminary Observations on TSA's Progress and Challenges in Meeting the Statutory Mandate for Screening Air Cargo on Passenger Aircraft, http://www.gao.gov/products/GAO-09-422T (Washington, D.C.: Mar. 18, 2009); Aviation Security: Vulnerabilities Exposed Through Covert Testing of TSA's Passenger Screening Process, http://www.gao.gov/products/GAO-08-48T (Washington, D.C.: Nov. 15, 2007); and Terrorist Watch List Screening: Opportunities Exist to Enhance Management Oversight, Reduce Vulnerabilities in Agency Screening Processes, and Expand Use of the List, http://www.gao.gov/products/GAO-08-110 (Washington, D.C.: Oct. 11, 2007).

tradeoffs between security, privacy, and the efficient flow of commerce. Striking the right balance between these three goals is an ongoing challenge facing TSA.

My testimony today focuses on (1) TSA's plans to procure, deploy, and test AITs to enhance the security of the passenger checkpoint, and any challenges TSA faces in this effort; and (2) TSA's efforts to strengthen screening procedures and technology in other areas of aviation security, and any related challenges the agency faces in these areas.

This statement is based on related GAO reports and testimonies we issued from March 2009 through January 2010, as well as preliminary observations based on ongoing work—from October 2008 through February 2010—to be completed later this year assessing the progress that DHS and its component agencies have made in addressing challenges related to air cargo security.[3] To conduct all of this work, we reviewed relevant documents related to the programs reviewed, and interviewed cognizant Department of Homeland Security (DHS) and TSA officials. All of this work was conducted in accordance with generally accepted government auditing standards, and our previously published reports contain additional details on the scope and methodology for those reviews. In addition, this statement contains selected updates conducted from December 2009 through March 2010 on TSA's effort to procure and deploy the AIT. For the updates, we obtained information from DHS and TSA on the AIT and interviewed senior TSA officials regarding the planned procurement, deployment, operational testing and evaluation, and assessment of benefits and costs of the AITs. We conducted these updates in accordance with generally accepted government auditing standards. Those standards require that we plan and perform the audit to obtain sufficient, appropriate evidence to provide a reasonable basis for our findings and conclusions based on our audit objectives. We believe that the evidence obtained provides a reasonable basis for our findings based on our audit objectives.

Background

Airline Passenger Screening Using Checkpoint Technology

Passenger screening is a process by which screeners inspect individuals and their property to deter and prevent an act of violence or air piracy, such as the carrying of any unauthorized explosive, incendiary, weapon, or other

---

[3] http://www.gao.gov/products/GAO-10-401T; http://www.gao.gov/products/GAO-10-128; http://www.gao.gov/products/GAO-10-106, and http://www.gao.gov/products/GAO-09-422T

prohibited item on board an aircraft or into a sterile area. Screeners inspect individuals for prohibited items at designated screening locations. TSA developed standard operating procedures for screening passengers at airport checkpoints. Primary screening is conducted on all airline passengers before they enter the sterile area of an airport and involves passengers walking through a metal detector, and carry-on items being subjected to X-ray screening. Passengers who alarm the walk-through metal detector or are designated as selectees—that is, passengers selected for additional screening—must then undergo secondary screening, as well as passengers whose carry-on items have been identified by the X-ray machine as potentially containing prohibited items. Secondary screening involves additional means for screening passengers, such as by hand wand; physical pat down; or other screening methods such as the AIT.

Role of DHS Science & Technology Directorate

Within DHS, both the Science and Technology Directorate (S&T) and TSA have responsibilities for researching, developing, and testing and evaluating new technologies, including airport checkpoint screening technologies. Specifically, S&T is responsible for the basic and applied research and advanced development of new technologies, while TSA, through its Passenger Screening Program (PSP), identifies the need for new checkpoint screening technologies and provides input to S&T during the research and development of new technologies, which TSA then procures and deploys. Because S&T and TSA share responsibilities related to the research, development, test and evaluation (RDT&E), procurement, and deployment of checkpoint screening technologies, the two organizations must coordinate with each other and external stakeholders, such as airport operators and technology vendors.

Air Cargo Security

Air cargo can be shipped in various forms, including unit load devices (ULD) that allow many packages to be consolidated into one container or pallet; wooden crates; or individually wrapped/boxed pieces, known as loose or break-bulk cargo. Participants in the air cargo shipping process include shippers, such as manufacturers; freight forwarders, who consolidate cargo from shippers and take it to air carriers for transport; air cargo handling agents, who process and load cargo onto aircraft on behalf of air carriers; and air carriers that load and transport cargo.[4] TSA's responsibilities

---

[4] For purposes of this statement, the term freight forwarders only includes those freight forwarders that are regulated by TSA, also referred to as indirect air carriers.

include, among other things, establishing security requirements governing domestic and foreign passenger air carriers that transport cargo and domestic freight forwarders.

Airport Perimeter Security and Access Control

Airport perimeter and access control security is intended to prevent unauthorized access into secured airport areas, either from outside the airport complex or from within. Airport operators generally have direct day-to-day responsibility for maintaining and improving perimeter and access control security, as well as implementing measures to reduce worker risk. However, TSA has primary responsibility for establishing and implementing measures to improve security operations at U.S. commercial airports—that is, TSA-regulated airports—including overseeing airport operator efforts to maintain perimeter and access control security.[5] Airport workers may access sterile areas through TSA security checkpoints or through other access points that are secured by the airport operator. The airport operator is also responsible, in accordance with its security program, for securing access to secured airport areas where passengers are not permitted. Airport methods used to control access vary, but all access controls must meet minimum performance standards in accordance with TSA requirements.

Increased Deployment of AIT Highlights the Importance of Operational Testing and Cost-Benefit Analysis Prior to Deployment

TSA Plans to Procure and Deploy 1,800 AITs by 2014 and Use Them as a Primary Screening Measure

In response to the December 2009 attempted terrorist attack, TSA has revised its procurement and deployment strategy for the AIT, increasing the number of AITs it plans to procure and deploy. In contrast with its prior strategy, the agency now plans to acquire and deploy 1,800 AITs (instead of the 878 units it had previously planned to acquire) and to use them as a primary screening measure where feasible rather than solely as a secondary screening measure. According to a senior TSA official, the agency is taking these actions in response to the Christmas Day 2009 terrorist incident.

---

[5] See generally Aviation and Transportation Security Act, Pub. L. No. 107-71, 115 Stat. 597 (2001).

These officials stated that they anticipate the AIT will provide enhanced security benefits compared to walk-through metal detectors, such as enhanced detection capabilities for identifying nonmetallic threat objects and liquids. TSA officials also stated that the AIT offers greater efficiencies because it allows TSA to more rigorously screen a greater number of passengers in a shorter amount of time while providing a detection capability equivalent to a pat down. For example, the AIT requires about 20 seconds to produce and interpret a passenger's image as compared with 2 minutes required for a physical pat down. A senior official also stated that TSA intends to continue to offer an alternative but comparable screening method, such as a physical pat down, for passengers who prefer not to be screened using the AIT.

The AIT produces an image of a passenger's body that a screener interprets. The image identifies objects, or anomalies, on the outside of the physical body but does not reveal items beneath the surface of the skin, such as implants. TSA plans to procure two types of AIT units: one type uses millimeter-wave and the other type uses backscatter X-ray technology. Millimeter-wave technology beams millimeter-wave radio-frequency energy over the body's surface at high speed from two antennas simultaneously as they rotate around the body. The energy reflected back from the body or other objects on the body is used to construct a three-dimensional image. Millimeter wave technology produces an image that resembles a fuzzy photo negative. Backscatter X-ray technology uses a low-level X-ray to create a two-sided image of the person. Backscatter technology produces an image that resembles a chalk etching.

As of February 24, 2010, according to a senior TSA official, the agency has deployed 40 of the millimeter-wave AITs and procured 150 backscatter X-ray units in fiscal year 2009. In early March 2010, TSA initiated the deployment of these backscatter units starting with two airports, Logan International Airport in Boston, Massachusetts, and Chicago O'Hare International Airport in Des Plaines, Illinois. TSA officials stated that they do not expect these units to be fully operational, however, until the second or third week of March due to time needed to hire and train additional personnel. TSA estimates that the remaining backscatter X-ray units will be installed at airports by the end of calendar year 2010. In addition, TSA plans to procure an additional 300 AIT units in fiscal year 2010, some of which it plans to purchase with funds from the American Recovery and Reinvestment Act of 2009. In fiscal year 2011, TSA plans to procure 503 AIT units. TSA projects that a total of about 1,000 AIT systems will be deployed to airports by the end of December 2011. In fiscal year 2014 TSA plans to reach full operating capacity, having procured a total of 1,800 units and deployed them to 60 percent of the checkpoint lanes at Category X, I, and II airports.[6] The current projected full operating capacity of 1,800 machines represents a more than two-fold increase from 878 units that TSA had previously planned. TSA officials stated that the cost of the AIT is about $170,000 per unit, excluding training, installation, and maintenance costs. In addition, in the fiscal year 2011 President's budget submission, TSA has requested $218.9 million for 3,550 additional full-time equivalents (FTE) to help staff the AITs deployed in that time frame. From 2012 through 2014, as TSA deploys additional units to reach full operating capacity, additional staff will be needed to operate these units; such staffing costs will recur on an annual basis. TSA officials told us that three FTEs are needed to operate each unit.

Because the AIT presents a full body image of a person during the screening process, concerns have been expressed that the image is an invasion of privacy. According to TSA, to protect passenger privacy and ensure anonymity, strict privacy safeguards are built into the procedures for use of the AIT. For example, the officer who assists the passenger does not see the image that the technology produces, and the officer who views the image is remotely located in a secure resolution room and does not see the passenger. Officers evaluating images are not permitted to take cameras, cell phones, or photo-enabled devices into the resolution room. To further protect passengers' privacy, ways have been introduced to blur the passengers' images. The millimeter-wave technology blurs all facial features, and the backscatter X-ray technology has an algorithm applied to the entire image to protect privacy. Further, TSA has stated that the AIT's capability to store, print, transmit, or save the image will be disabled at the factory before the machines are delivered to airports, and each image is automatically deleted from the system after it is cleared by the remotely located security officer. Once the remotely located officer determines that threat items are not present, that officer communicates wirelessly to the officer assisting the passenger. The passenger may then continue through the security process. Potential threat items are resolved through a directed physical pat down before the passenger is cleared to enter the sterile area.[7] In addition to privacy concerns, the AITs are large machines, and

---

[6] There are about 450 commercial airports in the United States. TSA classifies airports into one of five categories (X, I, II, III, and IV) based on various factors, such as the total number of takeoffs and landings annually, the extent to which passengers are screened at the airport, and other special security considerations. In general, category X airports have the largest number of passenger boardings, and category IV airports have the smallest.

[7] TSA stated that it continues to evaluate possible display options that include a "stick figure" or "cartoon-like" form to provide greater privacy protection to the individual being screened

adding them to the checkpoint areas will require additional space, especially since the operators are physically segregated from the checkpoint to help ensure passenger privacy. Adding a significant number of additional AITs to the existing airport infrastructure could impose additional challenges on airport operators.

TSA Recently Reported Efforts to Strengthen Its Operational Test and Evaluation Process, but It Is Not Clear Whether TSA Has Fully Evaluated the Relative Security Benefits and Costs of the AIT

In October 2009, we reported that TSA had relied on a screening technology in day-to-day airport operations that had not been proven to meet its functional requirements through operational testing and evaluation, contrary to TSA's acquisition guidance and a knowledge-based acquisition approach.[8] We also reported that TSA had not operationally tested the AITs at the time of our review, and we recommended that TSA operationally test and evaluate technologies prior to deploying them.[9] In commenting on our report, TSA agreed with this recommendation. Although TSA does not yet have a written policy requiring operational testing prior to deployment, a senior TSA official stated that TSA has made efforts to strengthen its operational test and evaluation process and that TSA is now complying with DHS's current acquisition directive that requires operational testing and evaluation be completed prior to deployment.[10] According to officials, TSA is now requiring that AIT are to successfully complete both laboratory tests and operational tests prior to deployment.

As we previously reported, TSA's experience with the explosives trace portal (ETP), or "puffers," demonstrates the importance of testing and evaluation in an operational environment.[11] The ETP detects traces of explosives on a

---

while still allowing the unit operator or automated detection algorithms to detect possible threats. DHS is working directly with technology providers to develop advanced screening algorithms for the AIT that would utilize Automatic Target Recognition to identify and highlight possible threats.

[8] http://www.gao.gov/products/GAO-10-128.

[9] Operational testing refers to testing in an operational environment in order to verify that new systems are operationally effective, supportable, and suitable.

[10] DHS Acquisition Management Directive 102-01, Jan. 20, 2010.

[11] We have previously reported that deploying technologies that have not successfully completed operational testing and evaluation can lead to cost overruns and underperformance. In addition, our reviews have shown that leading commercial firms follow a knowledge-based

passenger by using puffs of air to dislodge particles from the passenger's body and clothing that the machine analyzes for traces of explosives. TSA procured 207 ETPs and in 2006 deployed 101 ETPs to 36 airports, the first deployment of a checkpoint technology initiated by the agency.[12] TSA deployed the ETPs even though tests conducted during 2004 and 2005 on earlier ETP models suggested that they did not demonstrate reliable performance. Furthermore, the ETP models that were subsequently deployed were not tested to prove their effective performance in an operational environment, contrary to TSA's acquisition guidance, which recommends such testing. As a result, TSA procured and deployed ETPs without assurance that they would perform as intended in an operational environment. TSA officials stated that they deployed the machines without resolving these issues to respond quickly to the threat of suicide bombers. In June 2006 TSA halted further deployment of the ETP because of performance, maintenance, and installation issues. According to a senior TSA official, as of December 31, 2009, all but 9 ETPs have been withdrawn from airports, and 18 ETPs remain in inventory.

Following the completion of our review, TSA officials told us that the AIT successfully completed operational testing at the end of calendar year 2009 before its deployment was fully initiated. The official also stated that the AIT test results were provided and reviewed by DHS's Acquisition Review Board prior to the board approving the AIT deployment. According to TSA's threat assessment, terrorists have various techniques for concealing explosives on their persons, as was evident in Mr. Abdulmutallab's attempted attack on December 25, when he concealed an explosive in his underwear. While TSA officials stated that the laboratory and operational testing of the AIT included placing explosive material in different locations on the body,[13] it remains unclear whether the AIT would have been able to detect the weapon Mr. Abdulmutallab used in his attempted attack based on the preliminary TSA information we have received. We are in the process of reviewing these operational tests to assess the AIT's detection capabilities and to verify that TSA successfully completed operational testing of the AIT.

---

approach to major acquisitions and do not proceed with large investments unless the product's design demonstrates its ability to meet functional requirements and be stable. The developer must show that the product can be manufactured within cost, schedule, and quality targets and is reliable before production begins and the system is used in day-to-day operations. See http://www.gao.gov/products/GAO-10-128 and GAO, Best Practices: Using a Knowledge-Based Approach to Improve Weapon Acquisition, http://www.gao.gov/products/GAO-04-386SP (Washington, D.C.: Jan. 2004).

[12] TSA deployed the ETPs from January to June 2006.

[13] The results of TSA's laboratory and operational testing are classified.

In addition, while TSA officials stated that the AITs performed as well as physical pat downs in operational testing, TSA officials also reported they have not conducted a cost-benefit analysis of the original or revised AIT deployment strategy. We reported in October 2009 that TSA had not conducted a cost-benefit analysis of checkpoint technologies being researched and developed, procured, and deployed and recommended that it do so. DHS concurred with our recommendation. Cost-benefit analyses are important because they help decision makers determine which protective measures, for instance, investments in technologies or in other security programs, will provide the greatest mitigation of risk for the resources that are available. TSA officials stated that a cost-benefit analysis was not completed for the AIT because one is not required under DHS acquisition guidance. However, these officials reported that they had completed, earlier in the program, a life-cycle cost estimate and an analysis of alternatives for the AIT as required by DHS, which, according to agency officials, provides equivalent information to a cost-benefit analysis. We are in the process of reviewing the alternatives analysis that was completed in 2008 and life-cycle cost estimates which TSA provided to us on March 12, 2010, to determine the extent to which these estimates reflect the additional costs to staff these units. We estimate that, based on TSA's fiscal year 2011 budget request and current AIT deployment strategy, increases in staffing costs due to doubling the number of AITs that TSA plans to deploy could add up to $2.4 billion over the expected service life of this investment.[14]

While we recognize that TSA is taking action to address a vulnerability of the passenger checkpoint exposed by the December 25, 2009, attempted attack, we continue to believe that, given TSA's expanded deployment strategy, conducting a cost-benefit analysis of TSA's AIT deployment is important. An updated cost-benefit analysis would help inform TSA's judgment about the optimal deployment strategy for the AITs, as well as provide information to inform the best path forward, considering all elements of the screening system, for addressing the vulnerability identified by this attempted terrorist attack.

---

[14] To estimate the cost of the additional staff needed to operate the AIT machines during their service life as a result of TSA's increased deployment of the AIT, we used information in the President's Budget Request for Fiscal Year 2011 and from interviews with TSA officials. We identified staffing costs to operate each AIT ($369,764) and multiplied this figure by the number of additional AITs that TSA has recently planned to deploy by 2014 (922 units) to calculate the additional staffing costs, which equaled $340,922,408. We then multiplied the additional staffing costs of $340,922,408 by 7 years to calculate the additional staffing cost to operate additional AIT units during their expected service life, which equaled $2,386,456,856.

TSA Has Made Progress in Securing Air Cargo and Airport Access, but Challenges Remain

TSA Has Made Progress in Meeting the Air Cargo Screening Mandate, but Faces Participation, Technology, Oversight, and Inbound-Cargo Challenges

As we previously reported in March 2009, based on preliminary observations from ongoing work, TSA has taken several key steps to meet the statutory mandate to screen 100 percent of air cargo transported on passenger aircraft by August 2010.[15] Among the steps that TSA has taken to address domestic air cargo screening, the agency has revised its security programs to require more cargo to be screened; created the Certified Cargo Screening Program (CCSP), a voluntary program to allow screening to take place earlier in the shipping process and at various points in the air cargo supply chain—including before the cargo is consolidated; issued an interim final rule, effective November 16, 2009, that, among other things, codifies the statutory air cargo screening requirements of the 9/11 Commission Act and establishes requirements for entities participating in the CCSP;[16] established a technology pilot program to operationally test explosives trace detection (ETD) and X-ray technology;[17] and expanded its explosives detection canine program.

While these steps are encouraging, TSA faces several challenges in meeting the air cargo screening mandate. First, although industry participation in the CCSP is vital to TSA's approach to move screening responsibilities across the U.S. supply chain, the voluntary nature of the program may make it difficult to attract program participants needed to screen the required levels of

---

[15] GAO-09-422T. The Implementing Recommendations of the 9/11 Commission Act of 2007 (9/11 Commission Act) requires that by August 2010, 100 percent of cargo—domestic and inbound—transported on passenger aircraft be physically screened. The 9/11 Commission Act establishes minimum standards for screening air cargo and defines screening for purposes of the air cargo screening mandate as a physical examination or nonintrusive methods of assessing whether cargo poses a threat to transportation security. Solely performing a review of information about the contents of cargo or verifying the identity of the cargo's shipper does not constitute screening for purposes of satisfying the mandate. See Pub. L. No. 110-53, § 1602(a), 121 Stat. 266, 477-79 (codified at 49 U.S.C. § 44901(g)). For the purposes of this statement, domestic air cargo refers to cargo transported by air within the United States and from the United States to a foreign location by both U.S. and foreign-based air carriers; and inbound cargo refers to cargo transported by U.S. and foreign-based air carriers from a foreign location to the United States.

[16] See Air Cargo Screening, 74 Fed. Reg. 47672 (Sept. 16, 2009).

[17] ETD requires human operators to collect samples of items to be screened with swabs, which are chemically analyzed to identify any traces of explosives material.

domestic cargo. Second, while TSA has taken steps to test technologies for screening and securing air cargo, it has not yet completed assessments of the various technologies it plans to allow air carriers and program participants to use in meeting the August 2010 screening mandate. According to TSA officials, several X-ray and explosives detection systems (EDS) technologies successfully passed laboratory testing, and TSA placed them on a December 2009 list of qualified products that industry can use to screen cargo after August 2010.[18] TSA plans to conduct field testing and evaluation of these technologies in an operational environment. In addition, TSA plans to begin laboratory testing for ETD, Electronic Metal Detection (EMD), and additional X-ray technologies in early 2010, and anticipates including these technologies on the list of qualified products the industry can use by the summer of 2010, before proceeding with operational testing.[19] As we previously reported, based on preliminary observations from ongoing work, X-ray and ETD technologies, which have not yet been fully tested for effectiveness, are currently being used by industry participants to meet air cargo screening requirements.[20] We are examining this issue in more detail as part of our ongoing review of TSA's air cargo security efforts, to be issued later this year.

Third, TSA faces challenges overseeing compliance with the CCSP due to the size of its current Transportation Security Inspector (TSI) workforce. Under the CCSP, in addition to performing inspections of air carriers and freight forwarders, TSIs are to also perform compliance inspections of new regulated entities that voluntarily become certified cargo screening facilities (CCSF), as well as conduct additional CCSF inspections of existing freight forwarders. TSA officials have stated that the agency is evaluating the required number of TSIs to fully implement and oversee the program. Completing its staffing study may help TSA determine whether it has the necessary staffing resources to ensure that entities involved in the CCSP are meeting TSA requirements to screen and secure air cargo.[21] As part of our ongoing work, we are exploring to what extent TSA is undertaking a staffing study.

---

[18] EDS uses computer-aided tomography X-rays to examine objects inside baggage and identify the characteristic signatures of threat explosives.

[19] EMD devices are capable of detecting metallic-based explosives, such as wires, within a variety of perishable commodities at the cargo-piece, parcel, and pallet level.

[20] http://www.gao.gov/products/GAO-09-422T.

[21] For additional information on TSA's staffing study, see GAO, Aviation Security: Status of Transportation Security Inspector Workforce, http://www.gao.gov/products/GAO-09-123R (Washington D.C.: Feb. 6, 2009).

Finally, TSA has taken some steps to meet the screening mandate as it applies to inbound cargo but does not expect to achieve 100 percent screening of inbound cargo by the August 2010 deadline. TSA revised its requirements to, in general, require carriers to screen 50 percent of nonexempt inbound cargo. TSA also began harmonization of security standards with other nations through bilateral and quadrilateral discussions.[22] In addition, TSA continues to work with Customs and Border Protection (CBP) to leverage an existing CBP system to identify and target high-risk air cargo. However, TSA does not expect to meet the mandated 100 percent screening level by August 2010. This is due, in part, to challenges TSA faces in harmonizing the agency's air cargo security standards with those of other nations. Moreover, TSA's international inspection resources are limited. We will continue to explore these issues as part of our ongoing review of TSA's air cargo security efforts, to be issued later this year.

TSA Has Taken Actions to Strengthen Airport Security, but Faces Challenges That Include Assessing Risk and Evaluating Worker Screening Methods

In our September 2009 report on airport security, we reported that TSA has implemented a variety of programs and protective actions to strengthen the security of commercial airports.[23] For example, in March 2007, TSA implemented a random worker screening program—the Aviation Direct Access Screening Program (ADASP)—nationwide to enforce access procedures, such as ensuring that workers do not possess unauthorized items when entering secured areas.[24] In addition, TSA has expanded requirements for background checks and for the population of individuals who are subject to these checks, and has established a statutorily directed pilot program to assess airport security technology.[25]

As we reported in September 2009, while TSA has taken numerous steps to enhance airport security, it continues to face challenges in several areas, such

---

[22] The term harmonization is used to describe countries' efforts to coordinate their security practices to enhance security and increase efficiency by avoiding duplication of effort.

[23] GAO, Aviation Security: A National Strategy and Other Actions Would Strengthen TSA's Efforts to Secure Commercial Airport Perimeters and Access Controls, http://www.gao.gov/products/GAO-09-399 (Washington, D.C.: Sept. 30, 2009).

[24] For the purposes of this statement "secured area" is used generally to refer to areas specified in an airport security program that require restricted access. See 49 C.F.R. §§ 1540.5, 1542.201.

[25] According to TSA officials, the agency established this program in response to a provision enacted through the Aviation and Transportation Security Act. See Pub. L. No. 107-71 § 106(d), 115 Stat. at 610 (codified at 49 U.S.C. § 44903(c)(3)).

as assessing risk, evaluating worker screening methods, addressing airport technology needs, and developing a unified national strategy for airport security.[26] For example, while TSA has taken steps to assess risk related to airport security, it has not conducted a comprehensive risk assessment based on assessments of threats, vulnerabilities, and consequences, as required by DHS's National Infrastructure Protection Plan. To address these issues, we recommended, among other things, that TSA develop a comprehensive risk assessment of airport security and milestones for its completion, and evaluate whether the current approach to conducting vulnerability assessments appropriately assesses vulnerabilities. DHS concurred with these recommendations and stated that TSA is taking actions to implement them.

Our September 2009 report also reported the results of TSA efforts to help identify the potential costs and benefits of 100 percent worker screening and other worker screening methods.[27] In July 2009 TSA issued a final report on the results and concluded that random screening is a more cost-effective approach because it appears "roughly" as effective in identifying contraband items at less cost than 100 percent worker screening.[28] However, the report also identified limitations in the design and evaluation of the program and in the estimation of costs, such as the limited number of participating airports, the limited evaluation of certain screening techniques, the approximate nature of the cost estimates, and the limited amount of information available regarding operational effects and other costs. Given the significance of these limitations, we reported in September 2009 that it is unclear whether random worker screening is more or less cost effective than 100 percent worker screening. In addition, TSA did not document key aspects of the pilot's design, methodology, and evaluation, such as a data analysis plan, limiting the usefulness of these efforts. To address this, we recommended that TSA ensure that future airport security pilot program evaluation efforts include a well-developed and well-documented evaluation plan, to which DHS concurred.

---

[26] http://www.gao.gov/products/GAO-09-399.

[27] To respond to the threat posed by airport workers, the Explanatory Statement accompanying the DHS Appropriations Act, 2008, directed TSA to use $15 million of its appropriation to conduct a pilot program at seven airports. Explanatory Statement accompanying Division E of the Consolidated Appropriations Act, 2008, Pub. L. No. 110-161, Div. E, 121 Stat. 1844, 2042 (2007), at 1048. While the Statement refers to these pilot programs as airport employee screening pilots, for the purposes of this statement, we use "worker screening" to refer to the screening of all individuals who work at the airport.

[28] Transportation Security Administration, Airport Employee Screening Pilot Program Study: Fiscal Year 2008 Report to Congress (Washington, D.C., July 7, 2009).

Moreover, although TSA has taken steps to develop biometric worker credentialing, it is unclear to what extent TSA plans to address statutory requirements regarding biometric technology, such as developing or requiring biometric access controls at airports, establishing comprehensive standards, and determining the best way to incorporate these decisions into airports' existing systems.[29] To address this issue, we have recommended that TSA develop milestones for meeting statutory requirements for, among other things, performance standards for biometric airport access control systems. DHS concurred with this recommendation. Finally, TSA's efforts to enhance the security of the nation's airports have not been guided by a national strategy that identifies key elements, such as goals, priorities, performance measures, and required resources. To better ensure that airport stakeholders take a unified approach to airport security, we recommended that TSA develop a national strategy that incorporates key characteristics of effective security strategies, such as measurable goals and priorities, to which DHS concurred and stated that TSA is taking action to implement it.

Project Newton May Result in New Explosives Testing Standards for TSA's Screening Technology

As we discussed in our October 2009 report, TSA and the DHS Science and Technology Directorate (S&T) are pursuing an effort—known as Project Newton—which uses computer modeling to determine the effects of explosives on aircraft and develop new requirements to respond to emerging threats from explosives.[30] Specifically, TSA and S&T are reviewing the scientific basis of their current detection standards for explosives detection technologies to screen passengers, carry-on items, and checked baggage. As part of this work, TSA and S&T are conducting studies to update their understanding of the effects that explosives may have on aircraft, such as the consequences of detonating explosives on board an in-flight aircraft. Senior TSA and DHS S&T officials stated that the two agencies decided to initiate this review because they could not fully identify or validate the scientific support requiring explosives detection technologies to identify increasingly smaller amounts of some explosives over time as required by TSA policy. Officials stated that they used the best available information to originally

---

[29] Among other things, the Intelligence Reform and Terrorism Prevention Act of 2004 directed TSA, in consultation with industry representatives, to establish comprehensive technical and operational system requirements and performance standards for the use of biometric identifier technology in airport access control systems. See Pub. L. No. 108-458, § 4011, 118 Stat. 3638, 3712-14 (2004) (codified at 49 U.S.C. § 44903(h)(5)).

[30] http://www.gao.gov/products/GAO-10-128.

develop detection standards for explosives detection technologies. According to these officials, TSA's understanding of how explosives affect aircraft has largely been based on data obtained from live-fire explosive tests on aircraft hulls at ground level. Officials further stated that due to the expense and complexity of live-fire tests, the Federal Aviation Administration, TSA, and DHS collectively have conducted only a limited number of tests on retired aircraft, which limited the amount of data available for analysis. As part of this ongoing review, TSA and S&T are simulating the complex dynamics of explosive blast effects on an in-flight aircraft by using a computer model based on advanced software developed by the national laboratories. TSA believes that the computer model will be able to accurately simulate hundreds of explosives tests by simulating the effects that explosives will have when placed in different locations within various aircraft models. As discussed in our October 2009 report, TSA and S&T officials expect that the results of this work will provide a much fuller understanding of the explosive detection requirements and the threat posed by various amounts of different explosives, and will use this information to determine whether any modifications to existing detection standards should be made moving forward. We are currently reviewing Project Newton and will report on it at a later date.

Madame Chairwoman, that concludes my statement and I would be happy to answer any questions.

Contacts and Acknowledgments

For additional information about this statement, please contact Stephen M. Lord at (202) 512-4379 or lords@gao.gov. In addition to the contact named above, staff who made key contributions to this statement were E. Anne Laffoon and Steve D. Morris, Assistant Directors; Nabajyoti Barkakati, Carissa Bryant, Frances Cook, Joseph E. Dewechter, Amy Frazier, Barbara Guffy, David K. Hooper, Richard B. Hung, Lori Kmetz, Linda S. Miller, Timothy M. Persons, Yanina Golburt Samuels, Emily Suarez-Harris, and Rebecca Kuhlmann Taylor.

I

Index

CPSIA information can be obtained at www.ICGtesting.com
Printed in the USA
LVOW08s0526090114

368694LV00002B/449/P